Multiple Sclerosis

YOUR LEGAL RIGHTS

Multiple Sclerosis
YOUR LEGAL RIGHTS

THIRD EDITION

Lanny Perkins
Sara Perkins

Visit our web site at www.demosmedpub.com

LIBRARY OF CONGRESS CATALOGING-IN-PUBLICATION DATA
Perkins, Lanny E.
  Multiple sclerosis : your legal rights / Lanny Perkins, Sara Perkins. — 3rd ed.
    p. cm.
  Includes index.
  ISBN-13: 978-1-932603-63-7 (pbk. : alk. paper)
  ISBN-10: 1-932603-63-8 (pbk. : alk. paper)
  1. Multiple sclerosis—Patients—Legal status, laws, etc.—United States. I. Perkins, Sara. II. Title.
  KF3803.M84P47 2008
  346.7301'3—dc22

                                                                    2007048473

SPECIAL DISCOUNTS ON BULK QUANTITIES of Demos Medical Publishing books are available to corporations, professional associations, pharmaceutical companies, health care organizations, and other qualifying groups. For details, please contact:

> Special Sales Department
> Demos Medical Publishing
> 386 Park Avenue South, Suite 301
> New York, NY 10016
> Phone: 800–532–8663 or 212–683–0072
> Fax: 212–683–0118
> E-mail: orderdept@demosmedpub.com

MADE IN THE UNITED STATES OF AMERICA

07 08 09 10   5 4 3 2 1

Contents

Preface

WHY LANNY AND SARA PERKINS WROTE THIS BOOK

IN THE SPRING OF 1978 SARA WAS A FIRST-YEAR LAW student at Southern Methodist University School of Law. For most students the first year of law school is a stressful time. Professors, classmates, even your own spouse may create a lot of anxiety about performance. Around Easter, Sara noticed that she was experiencing painful vision and that the pages of her textbooks were blurred. Although it is not unusual for law students to get tired and frustrated, Sara finally went to her eye doctor, who referred her to a neuro-ophthalmologist. This doctor talked about "demyelinization." He told her the condition would probably pass and gave her a medication called prednisone. Sara did not think much more about it except for the problems she had in rescheduling her examinations.

Later in 1978 Lanny, then in a general law practice in a suburb of Dallas, Texas, was asked to represent a woman with multiple sclerosis (MS) who was being abandoned by her husband. Lanny knew very little about MS and vaguely thought that it might have something to do with the Jerry Lewis telethon. He did not associate it with any of the problems Sara had had earlier in the year.

By 1984 Sara had finished law school and was employed as a corporate attorney by a computer company in Dallas. One day in April of that year, she decided to go horseback riding. She came home complaining about dizziness and said that she had trouble staying on the horse. Sara went back to her doctor. She learned that she was probably having an attack of what was now identified as MS. Soon she began to have problems reading and staying awake through the workday. She often would close the door to her office and take a nap to hide her condition from her co-workers.

The same week Sara went to the doctor for the second time, Lanny took on a new client who was seeking disability benefits from Social Security. Her problem was a recurrence of MS.

Over the next year Sara attempted to continue working as before. Finally, in July 1985, she found it necessary to retire on disability. Lanny and Sara both became interested in MS, attempting to research medical journal articles and abstracts on new "breakthroughs," following attentively the progress of laboratory rats receiving drug therapies, and otherwise looking for medical panaceas.

They also got involved with the local National Multiple Sclerosis Society chapter. Sara did volunteer work and Lanny, who continued in private practice, accepted a number of MS patients as clients, with problems such as job discrimination, disability, and marital discord. Lanny and Sara were both asked to speak to support groups and at educational conferences around the state of Texas. In doing so, they became aware of the ways in which legal problems common to people with MS were influenced by the course of their medical condition.

They eventually prepared an outline of legal issues and approaches to solutions for publication. In 1988 that outline became the first edition of this book, *Multiple Sclerosis: Your Legal Rights*.

Since then Lanny and Sara have continued to work with individuals and advocacy groups to develop a better understanding of these issues. Changes in the law over the years have created more opportunities for people with MS. For instance, Sara was present in 1990 at the White House when President George Bush signed into law the Americans with Disabilities Act, which is discussed extensively in this volume. At the same time these new opportunities have also created more complex choices.

The objective of their new edition is to provide a source of basic information about legal problems that often affect people with MS and possible solutions to those problems. The authors address these issues at a level that is understandable by a lay audience. The previous editions, as well as this new edition will be helpful to people in supporting fields such as social workers, health care professionals, and lawyers who did not specialize in these areas.

It is not their intention to cause people to act as their own lawyers in complicated situations but to give them an overview of their problems so that they can decide when to seek professional advice. The book also provides frequent references to sources of legal assistance, both from private attorneys and from governmental and nonprofit agencies.

In the nearly 10 years from the second edition to this third edition of the book Sara's condition has significantly progressed. Changes in vision, walking, and energy levels have made daily life more difficult. This has greatly increased her interest in issues such as accessibility and drug costs. Fortunately, there are now resources available which can make our response to these kinds of problems more manageable. The more we learn about our rights and responsibilities under the law, the more useful we can be in our work, in our family life, and as citizens.

This third edition of *Multiple Sclerosis: Your Legal Rights* will help you learn about your rights and serve as a valuable resource no matter where you are in the disease process.

LANNY PERKINS
SARA PERKINS

Introduction

The more things change, the more they stay the same!

THERE HAVE BEEN MANY CHANGES IN THE MULTIPLE sclerosis (MS) and disability worlds since the last edition of this book was published. Some of the changes have been both good and bad, but it is important that people with MS are aware of them so they can better analyze what their options might be in certain circumstances.

Among the biggest changes are those dealing with the new Part D Medicare prescription benefit. This can present some real challenges for those people who are on or are thinking of taking the so-called A, B, C drugs as well as expensive medicines like natalizumab (Tysabri) and modafinil (Provigil).

Other important changes concern interpretations of the Americans with Disabilities Act (ADA) by the US Supreme Court. The ADA , signed into law in 1990, remains the bedrock of civil rights legislation in this country relating to the disabled. But because of its newness and complexity, its provisions are not always clear, and so will be a centerpiece of legal action for the foreseeable future.

Computers and the Internet were certainly around in 1999. Yet it is impossible to overemphasize their significance now. The resources are so varied that it is impossible to list them all. For example, people can compare the policies available to them in each state through Medicare Part D . It would be difficult to do this in any other way. The web does not answer every question, but it is a great tool to get a good deal of information quickly, especially for the physically challenged.

Some major areas of law such as bankruptcy and taxes need to be examined and updated. But the ways to think about and approach legal problems presented by the diagnosis of MS remain largely the same. This may be discouraging to some people, but it can also be empowering.

Multiple Sclerosis

YOUR LEGAL RIGHTS

I
Working with Doctors and Lawyers

MANY OF YOUR LEGAL AND FINANCIAL RIGHTS AS they relate to your medical condition may depend on the right choice of doctor and lawyer. These professionals can support or work for you and your best interests, so it is important to know why and how to hire—and fire—them.

THE DOCTOR

Most textbooks, pamphlets, and other written materials that deal with multiple sclerosis (MS) prudently counsel the individual to obtain good, regular medical care. Most doctors would advise the same. From there, sources differ. Some writers urge a team approach to treatment. Others suggest that a good general physician is adequate for ongoing treatment after an accurate diagnosis has been made. Sometimes the neurologist who has diagnosed is ready, willing, and able to monitor the patient regularly; sometimes the neurologist prefers to be involved only when there are exacerbations or serious new symptoms.

Whatever choice is made with regard to getting the best possible medical care, you should not overlook the importance your doctor may have in supporting you legally in such areas as insurance and Social Security claims, employment disputes, or legal competence issues. In addition to your hope that having the right doctor will help alleviate the physical effects of illness, having the right doctor also may greatly enhance your legal position in important ways; preferably before a crisis such as termination of employment occurs. The type of legal help a doctor most typically may provide includes writing clear statements as to the effects of your disease or giving written or oral testimony in support of a claim for a reasonable accommodation under the Americans with Disabilities Act (ADA) or for disability to insurers, employers, and the Social Security Administration (SSA).

In selecting a doctor, follow these tips:

1. Make sure that the doctor is interested in treating MS. Many doctors, even neurologists, for a wide variety of reasons, do not want to treat this condition.

2. See a neurologist or physiatrist (a physician whose specialty is physical medicine and rehabilitation) periodically. Many doctors, including neurologists, may say that it is not necessary to see a neurologist regularly, if ever, after diagnosis, but that a good internist is adequate. This may not be good legal advice if there is any likelihood that you will ever need medical evidence about your MS presented to a court or administrative agency. Because MS is a disease of the central nervous system, the opinion of a board-certified neurologist tends to be given greater weight by insurance companies, the SSA, and the courts. In fact, whenever a written report or affidavit is submitted in a legal or administrative proceeding, the doctor's accreditations should be fully listed in addition to his signature.

3. See the neurologist at least three or four times a year and also whenever there are new symptoms and exacerbations. Report all symptoms. Make sure the doctor is recording them in your file. This record of your progress will be the most important proof of your condition in any later legal or administrative proceedings, such as claiming disability benefits or proving medical expense tax deductions.

4. Keep an accurate diary of your symptoms and how they affect your activities, plus any other facts that you think are important. The purpose of this record is twofold. First, it will help you remember your own progress when consulting with your doctor. Second, it may be a significant piece of evidence of the effects of the disease on your life. The entries need not be extensive, but a consistently kept record is something that will enhance your medical, legal, and financial position in the face of an unpredictable illness.

5. Do not hesitate to discuss nonmedical issues with your doctor. In fact, do so as soon as possible. If you think the doctor will not be supportive, will not be willing to write appropriate documents or testify, and/or will not be willing to see you regularly, find a new doctor. Many doctors are sympathetic in the office but are reluctant to help a patient in nonmedical matters. This may be a major obstacle in some kinds of proceedings.

6. If you find out or suspect that your doctor is not sympathetic to either the medical or the nonmedical issues of MS, or for whatever reason you are not comfortable talking with him about those matters, how do you make a change? You may ask friends or other physicians for referrals. Another excellent source for finding doctors who are interested in MS is your local National Multiple Sclerosis Society (NMSS) chapter, which should provide several referrals (you generally must make the appointment).

7. Politely request a copy of your file from the doctor whose care you are leaving to avoid repeated testing and to give your new physician a copy of the case history. You are entitled to this copy on reasonable notice. There should be no problems with this request, but if the doctor refuses, your new doctor or the local county medical society should be able to help.

Of course, nowadays choosing a doctor is often made even more difficult because of the prevalence of HMOs (Health Maintenance Organizations) and PPOs (Preferred Provider Organizations). In many cases, you are under great pressure to accept the doctor assigned you by the HMO or to see someone from the favored list provided by the PPO. In many cases, these doctors are perfectly competent from a treatment point of view, but may or may not be willing to provide the kind of cooperation you need in coping with life problems of the type discussed in t book.

We will discuss medical insurance issues in Chapter 5 (Insurance Issues). But in making your selection of a treating doctor, it is important to bear in mind the possibility that you may need more than a 5-minute personal visit and a prescription at some point in your relationship.

If you take these considerations to heart after diagnosis, you may help yourself obtain the kind of support you deserve and need to deal with the complex legal issues to which a disease such as MS may give rise.

THE LAWYER

Many years ago, the *New Yorker* magazine published a cartoon that showed a fashionably dressed woman talking to a man at a cocktail party. The punch line read: "How did I know you're a lawyer? Everybody's a lawyer." Without question, there is no country in the world that has more lawyers per capita than the United States—now approximately 1 lawyer for every 350 people nationwide; perhaps 1 lawyer for every 20 people in Washington, DC, alone. But sheer volume does not mean it is easy to find the right lawyer for the particular legal problem you may have. Many people do not know any lawyers personally. There is, quite understandably, concern and confusion about such areas as specialization, fees, and competence.

The following points should give you some guidance.

1. One lawyer may not be able to address adequately all your legal problems, although the kind of extremely specialized practice often found in medicine is not quite as common in the law. Certain legal matters discussed here, such as divorce, probably can be handled well by any experienced civil practitioner. A good civil attorney should also be able to answer common questions concerning debt, real estate, and legally related business issues. However, that same attorney may know little about employment or Social Security but may be willing to learn about them in connection with a particular case. The problem, then, is at what cost in both money and ultimate result?

2. If you are concerned about a lawyer's experience or interest in handling a matter, first discuss it with the attorney by phone. You have no obligation to see that particular lawyer or any lawyer to whom you talk. However, if you make an appointment and do see the attorney, you may be charged for the visit whether or not you have her proceed with any other action, because the lawyer, like the physician, is selling you his time and knowledge.

3. It is perfectly acceptable and prudent to discuss fees with the lawyer by phone before you see her. In general, there are three basic methods of calculating fees: a contingency fee, meaning a percentage of money finally awarded or settled on in a case; hourly fees, which are based on the time spent on the legal matter; and a set fee for a particular job (e.g., $500 for a will or a simple divorce). Some kinds of legal problems typically are billed in a certain way. Personal injury and medical malpractice cases often are billed on a contingency basis, plus payment by the client of some costs such as court reporters, expert witness fees, and so forth. Other matters, such as divorce, might be billed as a set fee with some hourly billing if more than a given amount of time or effort is required. In these and other cases, a lawyer often will require a retainer to begin any work, bill against it, and, if necessary, bill the client for any additional time not covered by the retainer. Fees in some matters, such as worker's compensation and Social Security disability, are either set by statute or must be approved by a court or regulatory body.

A lawyer may ask you to sign a contract for services that sets forth the fee arrangement. This is not always done, but it is a practice of some lawyers, particularly in matters that might be expected to take a long time and involve a contingency fee.

Regardless of the type of case, a client should always understand in advance of commencing any legal action:

- What fees and charges may be expected.
- How much time will be involved.
- Who will be doing the work (the lawyer the client sees or someone else).
- What efforts are both the lawyer and the client expected to make.
- Any other issues that seem important to the client.

All good lawyers should be able to answer such questions clearly. If you understand from the outset what may be expected in your case, you will save yourself considerable anxiety, confusion, and possible expense in the future.

4. Before going to a lawyer, locate and take with you any documents, names, dates, addresses, or other information you deem to be important in your case. This may save the lawyer time and save you money.

5. Understand that however strong you believe your case is, you may not get the result you anticipate for many reasons other than poor performance by the lawyer. These might include a particular judge's or jury's peculiarities, the strength of the other side's case, or the economic constraints on your pursuing your case. The lawyer who tells you that you can either win or lose any disputed matter is only being honest.

6. There are several ways to find a lawyer who handles the matter you are interested in. Besides asking friends and acquaintances for names of competent attorneys who are interested in the legal problems of people with MS, one of the best sources of referral is the local bar association. In many cities and counties, bar associations sponsor lawyer referral services that will give you the name of a local lawyer who handles particular types of cases in your area of town. You may make an appointment to talk to the lawyer, often for a reduced price—a good value and a good way to get some basic questions answered even if you decide not to continue.

Other organizations in some parts of the country may offer similar services. You can find these in your telephone book. For example, one national referral service for attorneys who are interested in handling Social Security disability claims is the National Organization of Social Security Claimants' Representatives, which is headquartered in New Jersey (see the Appendix). Keep in mind that most referral services are just that—they give out names of lawyers who sign up and/or pay to be listed. They do not always indicate a lawyer's skills in a particular area of the law. Some state bar associations do provide board certifications, which may require a lawyer to have passed a written examination, to have a practice limited largely to the area of certification, to have been licensed for a minimum period of time, and to have submitted personal references from other attorneys.

7. Many organizations offer free or reduced-fee services to people who meet certain financial standards, normally involving low income levels. There may be other qualifications as well. For example, many law schools operate legal clinics for teaching purposes and are subject to certain restrictions on the type of cases handled. Further information on qualifications may be obtained directly from the organizations. Check your local telephone book. They may be of great use to those who qualify.

8. Legal guidebooks such as *The Martindale-Hubbell Law Digest* are available in local law and public libraries. These books list the names and addresses of law firms, along with biographic and other information (also see the Appendix). You should always meet with a lawyer before deciding to proceed with a major legal matter. Not only will you learn the anticipated legal steps and probable costs, but also a good attorney will give you an objective evaluation of your situation and some ideas about whether it is worthwhile to take the action you are considering. Of course, you should not necessarily follow the advice of the first lawyer you contact; lawyers, like doctors, may have different approaches to handling a given problem. In addition, you should try to hire a lawyer whose personality and philosophy will be compatible with yours, because the lawyer-client relationship must be one of mutual trust and confidence.

2
Making Choices About Employment and Income

The Fork in the Road

ONE OF THE MOST DIFFICULT AND FRUSTRATING aspects of dealing with multiple sclerosis (MS) is the question of whether and for how long you may expect to continue in your career, or whether at some point you may be forced to seek other sources of income such as disability benefits. The next several chapters discuss laws that may have an impact on this decision.

These subjects—employment discrimination, the availability of health and disability insurance, the workings of the Social Security Administration, and the like—should not be considered separately. Taken together, they may help you to look at all your options and how those options may be affected by changes in your medical condition.

For some reason, people with MS seem particularly disposed to a personality type that often includes a strong commitment to working and remaining financially independent. Sometimes this personality, when coupled with common MS symptoms, may come into conflict with the demands of the workplace. As a result, people may face what they perceive to be discrimination and lack of sympathy by their employers. Or they may genuinely have difficulty coping with the pressures that characterize many jobs today. And, of course, discrimination and unfair treatment occur all the time.

Many people find their entire lifestyle, including their sense of self-worth, bound up in their jobs and careers. This may render the problems of dealing with workplace demands all the more difficult. Another complication with MS is its often relapsing-remitting nature, which leads to uncertainties in predicting how your condition is likely to progress a few months, much less a few years, in the future.

For all these reasons, people with MS sometimes have to make what we call a "fork in the road" analysis of employment, disability, and other income-related matters. This refers to the fact that the legal standards that govern whether there may be a remedy for job discrimination under laws such as the Americans with Disabilities Act (ADA), which is discussed in Chapter 3, may lead us in a different direction than when we are considering the availability of private or Social Security disability benefits (see Chapter 4).

As you will see in our discussion of the ADA, if someone believes he has suffered employment discrimination, that person usually will need to be able to establish that he is still fully capable of doing his job despite his MS or other medical conditions. At the same time, the worker must be aware that should he decide that seeking Social Security or private disability benefits is in his future, the facts he must then prove, such as the severity of MS symptoms or the impossible demands of the job, might be just the reverse of those he would need to show in order to keep that same job under the ADA.

Therefore, workers with MS who are experiencing problems may have to decide whether they want to put together the necessary evidence from their doctors, their co-workers, performance evaluations, and other sources to prove their *ability* to do the job, or instead use those same factors to prove *disability*.

None of these choices is necessarily irrevocable, but it could be that choosing the wrong course, in hindsight, will make it more difficult to change directions at some point down the road. Once you have applied for and received Social Security disability benefits, it may be much harder both legally and—perhaps just as important—psychologically, to return to work and demonstrate that you can perform the kind of job you had before the period of disability. On the other hand, taking aggressive action to prove that your illness in no way handicaps you in your work performance may make it harder later on to show your entitlement to benefits. This is especially true if you lose the opportunity to apply for private disability benefits as a result of a delay in claiming disability. There also may be problems with the timing of the claim for Social Security disability benefits, particularly if the person has left the work force for an extended time. This is discussed in more detail in Chapter 4.

It is impossible to give specific advice as to what course readers should select for their own situation. It is important, however, that people with MS be aware of the choices before them, along with their costs and benefits. Perhaps the best way to ensure that you take the right "fork in the road" is to seek good information and advice from many different sources.

Here are some of the steps you may take to help you keep control over some of these important decisions, preferably before a crisis occurs:

1. Talk to your doctor about how he thinks your symptoms might develop and how they might affect your ability to do your job, including any side effects of medications you may need to take (see Chapter 1, Working with Doctors and Lawyers). Find out if this doctor is going to support you, either in trying to stay employed or in trying to seek disability benefits, if necessary. If not, find a new doctor.

2. Consult with a lawyer who has experience with employment and disability issues (again, see Chapter 1). Usually the sooner you talk to a good lawyer, the more help he can give you in avoiding legal problems or in dealing with them as they arise.

3. Get some help in planning your financial future. This may involve talking to an accountant or financial planner, or it may be enough simply to sit down with your spouse over the kitchen table and work out a budget. You may discuss such things as how to set aside money, whether you have any uninsured medical expenses, what to do about temporary loss of income if you have to quit one job to seek another with better benefits, or how you will manage until you start to receive disability payments.

4. Talk to other family members and friends about the support you may need—emotional, physical, and financial. This may include some very practical questions such as who can help you in dealing with the demands of your job and your illness by picking up the kids from school, accompanying you to medical appointments, or pitching in around the house.

5. You may want to talk to your employer, as is discussed in Chapter 3. The employer may have concerns of her own regarding job performance, insurance liability, and other matters. You should try to be clear in your own mind what you want before you have this conversation.

6. Above all, consult with yourself. You should look at yourself as objectively as possible and decide what your highest priorities are in terms of income, self-worth, and life goals. You may find the need to redefine a few things about yourself and, if you do, this could be the most important and certainly the most beneficial aspect of the experience.

The baseball great Yogi Berra had words of wisdom about these kinds of decisions, as about most things. He said "When you come to a fork in the road, take it."

Taking these steps will help you maintain control over your life so that you will feel confident with whatever decisions you make. Given our changing economy, the unpredictability of medical science, and the general uncertainty of life, that is probably as much as anyone can aim for.

3
Multiple Sclerosis and Your Job

MOST PEOPLE ARE DIAGNOSED WITH MULTIPLE sclerosis (MS) when they are still young and thinking about building a career. In some cases, early symptoms of MS—vision problems, fatigue—have already shown themselves in the workplace. Sometimes a person has written off these problems to "overwork" or "job stress." Now the worker is told that he has a chronic and currently incurable disease. How is this person's condition going to affect her ability to continue working? Although statistics in the medical and social literature show that perhaps 70 percent to 90 percent of all individuals with MS do some kind of work, it would be unrealistic to suggest that there will not be problems in getting and keeping a job, even for those people who think they are physically able to do so.

SHOULD YOU TELL YOUR BOSS?

One of the first employment issues relating to MS must be disclosure—should the employer be told of the existence of the disease? Most of us, of course, want to be honest and let our co-workers know what we are going through, what may have been causing us to behave differently at work, possibly to miss days, and perhaps we hope for a little support from those around us. However, we also are concerned that employers and co-workers may treat us differently, lose some confidence in our ability, and even deny us employment, promotion, or equal treatment. So the question arises—to tell or not to tell?

Sometimes the decision is made for you. The employer knows there is a problem through insurance claims, visual observation, or office gossip. Other times the issue may be more difficult. Should you disclose your diagnosis in an interview, in a health questionnaire, or during a preemployment physical? Should you disclose the diagnosis if you have few or no symptoms that are visible to others? What happens if you lie and are found out? You need to be aware of your own legal responsibilities and those of your present or potential employers.

In no case should you lie on an application or insurance form, because that may leave you open to later disciplinary measures, such as loss of a job or coverage. But consider carefully whether to volunteer information about your condition if it is not specifically asked about by the employer.

In an application form or preemployment interview, an employer may not directly ask an applicant if he is disabled or about the extent of any suspected disability. But the employer may ask if the applicant can perform the functions of a particular job. If a disability is known to the employer, the applicant may be asked how she can perform those job duties the employer believes may pose a problem and whether any adjustment in the job duties—an "accommodation"—will be needed. An employer may require a preemployment medical examination as a condition of a job offer, but this is permitted only if all applicants for the same job are required to undergo such an examination. That is, it may not be used as a way to screen out the disabled.

After employment, medical examinations must be job related and necessary for the conduct of business. The Americans with Disabilities Act, which is discussed in the subsequent section, imposes strict rules for the confidential maintenance of all medical records.

If the applicant is subsequently excluded from employment or is offered a different job based on the results of the examination, it must be because his limitations would not allow him to perform the essential functions of the job, even with reasonable accommodation.

However, it is sadly true that, despite laws intended to protect you, some employers or insurers may discriminate against you when you tell the truth— just because something is forbidden by law does not mean it cannot occur. Discrimination against the disabled—or those perceived as being disabled— does exist in this society. As companies become more and more concerned with insurance costs of all kinds—worker's compensation, health, disability—many are reluctant to hire or retain potentially costly "liabilities." Benevolent employers do exist, but an individual with MS would be well advised to consider the realities of human nature and the marketplace before volunteering information to prospective employers, current employers, and co-workers.

How to Protect Yourself from Discrimination

It is against both federal and state laws to discriminate against people with disabilities in employment. The two major federal laws are the Americans with Disabilities Act and the earlier Rehabilitation Act of 1973. These two acts overlap in many areas, but each is intended to provide protection on the job. Most states also have legislation dealing with employment discrimination against people with disabilities.

The Americans with Disabilities Act

When it was signed into law on July 26, 1990, the Americans with Disabilities Act (ADA) (42 USC 12101 *et seq.*) was widely heralded as the most significant civil rights legislation in a generation and as the world's first comprehensive civil rights law for people with disabilities. Not surprisingly, a law that is so ambitious is long and complex. Building on the foundation of earlier laws, principally the Civil Rights Act of 1964 and the Rehabilitation Act of 1973, the ADA prohibits discrimination on the basis of disability in employment, state and local government activities, public accommodations, commercial facilities, and telecommunications. Fortunately, the basic provisions are easy to grasp. Additionally, many resources are readily available, often free of charge, to explain ADA requirements in greater detail, including enforcement standards.

The ADA protects both people with disabilities and those who have a relationship or association with an individual with a disability. Under the general definitions of the ADA:

the term "disability" means, with respect to an individual—

(A) a physical or mental impairment that substantially limits one or more of the major life activities of such individual;

(B) a record of such an impairment; or

(C) being regarded as having such an impairment.

Although multiple sclerosis is not specifically listed in this definition or in Title I, the section that deals with employment, there is no doubt that MS is a physical impairment under the ADA. "Major life activities" include walking, seeing, hearing, standing, talking, learning, and working, among others. These are all the kinds of activities that may be affected by MS. "Impairment" *does not* mean that someone must use a wheelchair or be bedridden.

Under sections B and C, it may be that a person who has been given a diagnosis of MS but who is believed to be in remission would also be protected on the grounds that a history of MS symptoms could create a perception that would result in unfair discrimination.

What Is Discrimination?

Title I of the ADA prohibits discrimination in employment against a qualified individual with a disability. Employers who have 15 or more employees are covered by the Act. This does not mean that employers must employ individuals just because they have a disability. It does mean that qualified individuals with a disability must be given an equal opportunity to participate in all the employment practices that are available to nondisabled persons. These include applying for a job, hiring, firing, promotion, compensation, training, and other terms, conditions, and benefits of employment. Religious organizations that have more than 15 employees are also subject to Title I, although not to certain other requirements of the ADA.

A "qualified individual with a disability" is a person who meets all legitimate skill, educational, and other requirements for a position he seeks or holds and who can perform the "essential functions" of the job with or without "reasonable accommodation." What are the essential functions of a job? This provision is often a point of disagreement between an employer and the person with a disability. Essential functions are not minimal or marginal duties or tasks that are not likely to be called for in a particular job. For example, an accountant would not likely need to lift 50-pound weights. But what if she is required to put in long hours during tax season? ADA guidelines provide some examples of permissible and impermissible job requirements. But, as the regulations make clear, a case by case analysis is required to determine what is or is not "essential" in the context of discrimination under the ADA. This means that a person who believes he has been discriminated against may need legal advice to sort through the facts of a given situation.

Reasonable Accommodation

Even if the person with MS has some work limitation, that person may still be entitled to consideration for a given job if he can perform the essential duties with a "reasonable accommodation" by the employer. What is meant by "reasonable accommodation?" It means a modification or adjustment to a job or worksite that will allow a qualified applicant or employee with a disability to have privileges equal to those of nondisabled employees. For example, a desk may need to be raised so that a person in a wheelchair can sit in front of a computer. Examinations, training, and other activities may need to be modified so that a disabled person can compete equally. A worker who develops a disability that makes it impossible to perform her original job may have to be reassigned to another job that she is qualified to do. Time schedules may need to be altered to accommodate a worker's condition. This last example sounds like one that would be appropriate for many people with MS. But note: in a 1997 case decided by the Fifth Circuit Court of Appeals, the city of Dallas, Texas, did not have to accommodate an electrical inspector with MS who requested that her schedule be rearranged so she could arrive at work slightly later in the morning, because all city inspectors were required to be at the phones at a certain hour to receive calls from contractors. The judges questioned whether she could, in fact, perform the essential functions of the job. This was not, strictly speaking, an ADA case because it was brought under the earlier Rehabilitation Act of 1973, but the reasoning for the decision was similar to that which might be applied to the ADA. Each case must be analyzed on its own merits. There is no one-size-fits-all pattern. Employers are not required to lower their standards. The basic issue is whether an accommodation will allow the disabled person to perform a particular job.

There are limits on accommodations. The disability must be known to the employer. This may present problems, especially for people with a disease such as MS, which often is "hidden." The regulations envision that the disabled person will know what, if any, accommodation she needs or can come to an agreement with the employer, or that both will know to seek outside expertise.

Title I does not require reasonable accommodation for someone who is not disabled but who has a relationship with a disabled individual, such as the worker-spouse of a person with MS who wants time off to care for the MS spouse. Other laws, most notably the Family and Medical Leave Act (FMLA) and its state counterparts, may have the effect of requiring this kind of "accommodation" (see following section).

Undue Hardship

The ADA does not require an employer to undertake an "action requiring significant difficulty or expense" to accommodate a qualified individual with a disability when to do so would create an "undue hardship" in terms of factors such as cost, structure of operations, resources, and so forth. Most accommodations are not very expensive; for example, raising a desk to permit a person in a wheelchair to work comfortably, restructuring a job so that nonessential functions are assigned to other workers, or providing special parking spaces. In general, the larger an employer, the less burden an accommodation will present. Even if the cost of an accommodation would prove to be an undue hardship, the employer may still have to provide it if funding is available from other sources such as tax credits (see following section), state vocational rehabilitation funds, or even from the disabled individual herself in whole or in part. The ADA requires more than accommodations to a disabled employee's immediate worksite. In order to be able to equally participate in all activities of employment, other parts of the facility must be accessible. So unless there is an undue hardship, break rooms, cafeterias, gyms, and the like used by nondisabled employees would have to be modified, relocated, or created. A fundamental goal of the law is to end segregation on the basis of disability.

Under the ADA, an employer may set forth safety standards to exclude individuals who pose a direct significant risk to the health and safety of that individual or others unless the risk can be eliminated through reasonable accommodation. These standards must be based on objective evidence. For example, it is not enough that an employer *believes* that a person with MS will be a risk in an emergency because he may not be able to exit the workplace as quickly as other employees.

Help for the Employer

The costs of making some kinds of accommodations may be significant, especially for smaller companies. For that reason, Congress enacted two provisions in the tax code, sections 44 and 190, which may allow tax deductions and tax credits for the costs of providing various kinds of accommodations for disabled employees. These tax provisions might be a point to raise in discussing an accommodation with an employer, especially a small business that might be particularly affected by them but might not be familiar with their applicability (see Chapter 5).

Protection for Family Members

Another important provision of Title I bans discrimination on the basis of "relationship or association with an individual with a disability." This means that an employee who has a spouse with MS would be protected under the ADA in the same way as the individual with a disability is protected. For example, an employer could not fail to hire, fire, or promote for fear that the employee will be unable to perform the essential functions of the job because he may have to be absent at some point to care for his spouse, or that the MS spouse may raise the employer's insurance costs. This may become a significant protection when issues such as family leave or health insurance are concerned.

The Rehabilitation Act of 1973

The Rehabilitation Act of 1973 (Rehab Act) (29 USC 790 *et seq.*) bans discrimination on the basis of disability by federal contractors and by employers who receive federal financial assistance. It also bans discrimination in employment and requires affirmative action in agencies of the federal government. In some situations, both the Rehab Act and the ADA may apply, although you may not get "double" recovery of damages. Seek legal counsel for how to proceed with a complaint.

The Rehab Act defines an individual with a disability as:

> . . . any person who (i) has a physical or mental impairment which substantially limits one or more of such person's major life activities, (ii) has a record of such an impairment, or (iii) is regarded as having such an impairment.

Although the Rehab Act originally used the word *handicap* instead of *disability*, it was later amended to bring it into conformity with the language of the ADA.

Section 501 of the Rehab Act protects federal workers from discrimination on the basis of disability.

Under Section 503 of the Rehab Act, federal contractors must take affirmative action to accommodate the mental and physical limitations of an applicant or employee unless such accommodation imposes an undue hardship on the employer. There is no requirement that an employer meet hiring quotas or hire an unqualified worker.

Section 504 of the Rehab Act prohibits discrimination against a "qualified individual" in any program or activity that receives federal financial assistance or that is run by the federal government. Although each federal agency has its own 504 regulations and is responsible for enforcing the Act in the programs it administers, most requirements are similar.

As with the ADA, just what constitutes undue hardship has been a central issue in numerous cases brought under the Rehab Act. But in many situations, such accommodations as job reassignment, part-time work, redesigned work schedules, and providing readers and special equipment have been deemed to be reasonable accommodations.

Both the US House of Representatives and the Senate and their agencies are covered by the ADA. Federal government workers are covered by the Rehabilitation Act of 1973, with the standards for employment discrimination the same as Title I of the ADA.

What If You Need to Take Time Off?

So far, we have been talking mostly about how you can stay on the job despite having MS. However, there may come a time when you need to take time off from work to cope with symptoms of a severe exacerbation or to undertake a new course of treatment. You may need to extend your leave beyond that provided by your employer through the normal sick leave policy.

It is possible that some changes in your work hours or adjustment in your regular vacation schedule may be considered part of the reasonable accommodation your employer should make to you under the ADA, although there probably are significant limits on how far the courts will go in creating special time-out provisions because of your disability. After all, the employer may argue that the job still has to be done by somebody, and he cannot fairly be asked to pay your salary while also paying a replacement worker for an extended period of time.

It may also be that the spouse of the person with MS is the one who needs to take time off to allow her to lend a hand in dealing with trips to the doctor, household chores, or child care.

In these circumstances, a law enacted in 1993 called the Family and Medical Leave Act of 1993 (FMLA or the Act) (29 USC 2601 *et seq.*) may help. Strictly speaking, FMLA is not a "disability" law. It was intended to give eligible workers some assurance that in the event of a health care emergency, they would not have to choose between their job and their personal or family obligations. For employers, it was expected to promote a stable, productive work force. In any case, the Act may be extremely useful to a worker with MS and/or to a spouse, parent, or child with MS.

Like the ADA, the FMLA and its regulations are extensive, but the basic features are fairly straightforward. Title I applies to private sector employers, public agencies, and certain federal employers such as the US Postal Service. The Wage and Hour Division of the US Department of Labor's Employment Standards Administration regulates Title I. Title II of the FMLA, with similar provisions, covers most federal workers and is administered by the US Office of Personnel Management.

WHO IS ELIGIBLE FOR FAMILY LEAVE?

First, an employee must work for an employer who is covered by the FMLA. Private sector employers who have 50 or more employees on the payroll during 20 or more calendar workweeks in the current or preceding calendar year are covered. Part-time workers and those on leave are included in this total. Public employers and public and private schools are covered irrespective of number of employees. Although the Labor Department estimates that only 5 percent of private employers are subject to the FMLA, this still means that approximately 50 million workers in the United States are covered.

An "eligible employee" must have worked for the employer for at least 12 months (total time, not necessarily continuously or consecutively), with at least 1,250 hours of service before beginning the leave. Furthermore, the employee must be working at a site where the employer has at least 50 workers employed within a 75-mile radius.

The application of these statutory requirements may become rather confusing, but a rule of thumb is that you need to have worked 12 months for one employer at a site with a fair number of co-workers. Usually this will be readily apparent—for example, a branch bank may only have 15 full-time and part-time workers, but there are nine other branches in town. It also is conceivable that in some remote locations, a very large company might only have a few workers within 75 miles of each other. In general, under the FMLA, "eligible employees" may take up to a total of 12 workweeks of unpaid leave during any 12-month period for the birth, placement, or adoption of a child (men as well as women are eligible for FMLA leave for the birth of a child); to care for a spouse, parent (but not parent-in-law), or child with a serious health condition (under age 18 years unless disabled and incapable of self-care); or to care for the employee's own serious health condition. The Act provides the employer with several methods for choosing how to compute the "12-month period" in which the 12 weeks of leave may be taken. These include a calendar year, any fixed 12-month period such as a fiscal year or an employee's anniversary date, a 12-month period measured backward from the time an employee takes any family leave, or a 12-month period measured forward from the date an employee's first leave begins. Whatever method is adopted by an employer must be applied uniformly to all eligible employees.

The Act defines a "serious health condition" as an illness, injury, impairment, or physical or mental condition that involves inpatient care or continuing treatment by a health care provider. Although not specifically mentioned, MS could be a serious chronic or episodic condition that would give rise to rights under the FMLA. An employee who needs to be absent from work to receive medical treatment or to recover from an exacerbation, therefore, would be entitled to leave when she can no longer perform the essential functions of her job according to the ADA's definition of physical or mental impairment, which the FMLA adopts for this purpose. This situation is a good example of the interconnections between the FMLA and the ADA. Under the FMLA, however, leave is viewed not as an accommodation, but as an entitlement.

Leave does not need to be taken all at once or in the full 12-week allotment. In fact, one of the key features of the FMLA from the standpoint of someone with MS, or someone who may need to assist a family member with MS, is that leave may be taken in parts, on a reduced leave schedule (meaning a reduction in the usual number of hours worked by an employee per week or per day), intermittently, and over an extended period of time. In the case of a chronic serious health condition of an employee or family member, intermittent leave may be permitted even if there is no medical treatment being given; with the proper medical certification, personal and psychologic as well as physical care for a family member who is unable to care for himself may be a valid reason for leave. Two key points about a reduced leave schedule or intermittent leave must be mentioned:

1. Employees must try to arrange their leave to be as nondisruptive to employer operations as possible.

2. Subject to certain laws and conditions, an employer may temporarily assign an employee to an alternative job with equivalent pay and benefits but not necessarily equivalent duties.

Employers are required to maintain any preexisting group health insurance during the leave and, when the leave is concluded, to reinstate the employee to the same or an equivalent job with equivalent pay and benefits. If the employee was paying for all or part of his insurance before the leave, he must continue to pay for it during the leave. The employer may recover any portion it paid during the leave if the employee does not return to work except when this is due to factors beyond the employee's control; for example, the continuation of the serious medical condition. Continuation of health coverage mandated by the Consolidated Budget Reconciliation Act of 1985, or COBRA, (see Chapter 5) is independent of FMLA. That is, taking FMLA leave does not trigger a so-called "qualifying event" under the COBRA law. But if an eligible employee (or the spouse or dependent child) is covered by a group health plan through the employer, does not return to work at the end of FMLA leave, and has no other group health coverage, COBRA requirements would come into play. (Note: employers and plan administrators must comply with notice requirements; *employees also must elect COBRA coverage in a timely way*.)

FMLA leave generally is unpaid, although in some instances, paid vacation, personal, and medical/sick leave may be substituted for FMLA leave. When paid time off is still available, either the employer or the employee may choose to substitute paid leave for unpaid leave.

An employer has a right to 30 days advance notice of leave when practicable. This notice may be verbal or written and does not have to mention the FMLA. The employer may require a certification of medical need when the leave is due to a serious health problem (see certification form WH-380 at the end of this chapter). Failure to comply may result in denial of the leave. When the leave is due to the employee's own health problem, the employer may require another certification of fitness to return to work at the end of the leave period. Failure to supply such a certification may result in the employee's being denied reinstatement. But following ADA regulations, a return-to-work physical or certification must be job related. The employee generally must pay for this certification.

An employer may require an employee on leave periodically to report on her status and intent to return to work. If an employee gives notice that he does not intend to return, the employer is no longer obligated to provide health benefits (subject to COBRA rules). The employee's job is no longer protected. However, if an employee indicates that it may be impossible to return to work at the end of the leave, but that she still hopes to do so, FMLA protections and benefits should continue.

Employers subject to the Act must prominently post notices of its provisions (see sample Notice from the Labor Department at the end of the chapter). They also may have to explain the FMLA in other places where they describe employee benefits, such as in employee manuals. Records of eligibility must be maintained by the employer and are subject to Labor Department review. Any medical records related to the FMLA must be kept confidential and separate from other personnel information.

It is the employer's responsibility to provide written notice to the employee that the leave is being counted as FMLA leave (see Appendix). This notice should set out employee rights and obligations such as using accrued paid leave, obtaining medical certifications, and methods for paying insurance premiums. The notice should be provided within 2 business days of the employer's receiving a request for leave. Similarly, when an employer was not made aware that a leave qualified under the FMLA and the employee wants the time counted under the Act, the employee generally has 2 business days after returning to work to so notify the employer.

There are special FMLA rules for certain kinds of employees. "Key employees" are the highest paid 10 percent of employees within a 75-mile radius. When an employer determines that it will suffer "substantial and grievous economic injury" in restoring the worker to her job, the employer must inform a key employee that she will not be allowed back to work at the end of proposed leave and must give the employee a reasonable time to return. Teachers who take intermittent leave or who depart close to the end of a school term may be subject to restrictions on the length of personal leave or may be temporarily transferred to other jobs. Key employees and teachers are still entitled to leave, but with these and other limitations.

FMLA and Other Disability Laws

Although in some of its provisions, the FMLA uses ADA definitions, FMLA's "serious health condition" and ADA's "disability" are different concepts and are related to different legal goals. Because a person with MS who works may be protected under both laws at the same time, it is important carefully to analyze how to make the best use of the protections and benefits that each provides.

Whether an employee is considered to have an ADA disability or not, if he is "eligible" under the FMLA, he must be allowed 12 weeks of leave in a 12-month period. The ADA, on the other hand, may permit an indeterminate period of leave to a disabled worker as part of a reasonable accommodation, assuming no undue hardship for the employer. A kind of "permanent" leave under the ADA might be a part-time job. Although this may be desirable in some instances, the employer who does not offer health benefits to part-time workers would not have to provide them as an ADA accommodation. Under FMLA, an employer must maintain group health benefits during a leave subject to the same conditions as if the employee were still on the job.

When FMLA leave is taken as a reduced leave schedule, the employer may temporarily transfer the worker to an alternate job. Under the ADA, such a transfer may take place only if the employee cannot perform the essential functions of his present job and no other accommodation is possible.

If you can perform the essential functions of your current job but need a leave of a few weeks to recover from an exacerbation, it may make sense to request FMLA leave and its continued health benefits. The risk of involuntary transfer should be considered. On the other hand, if the time has come for more extensive job restructuring, such as part-time work, perhaps ADA would be a better choice. A middle ground, especially in light of the unpredictability of both MS and the effects of any course of drug therapy, might be to think of the leave as *both* an ADA accommodation *and* FMLA leave.

The following may help illustrate the possible interworkings of the ADA and the FMLA. Suppose that someone who is a qualified individual with a disability under the ADA and also an eligible employee under the FMLA requests leave as a medical accommodation. This is not an undue hardship, so it is granted by the employer, who tells the employee that it also will be counted as FMLA leave. Under this arrangement, at the end of the leave the ADA would require reinstatement to the *same* job (as opposed to an "equivalent" position under FMLA) provided the employee can perform all essential duties with or without reasonable accommodation; in the meantime, FMLA health benefits would continue in any case. Note: in many jobs, benefits would continue anyway during a short-term disability period, so that an ADA accommodation leave might not present any special benefits problems.

Suppose then that the employee returns to work before the end of the full 12-week FMLA entitlement but only on a part-time basis (reduced leave schedule). FMLA health benefits would continue for the remainder of the 12 weeks even if the employer does not provide such coverage to other part-time workers. The ADA protects the employee from involuntary temporary transfer to another job, unlike the FMLA in the case of an intermittent or reduced leave schedule.

At the end of FMLA leave, the employer is required only to reinstate the worker to the same or an equivalent job. If the worker cannot perform the essential functions of the job and if she is protected by the ADA, part-time work or posting to another job may represent a reasonable accommodation, assuming it is not an undue hardship. In no event does the ADA permit an employer to force a worker to accept a "reasonable accommodation" to avoid granting FMLA leave.

It is the *employer* who designates a leave as an FMLA leave. This does not mean that you have to give up any benefits or protections to which you are entitled under other laws. In fact, you are always entitled to the greatest protections provided by any applicable employment laws, state or federal. So if a state requires a comparable leave period with 16 weeks of benefits, an employer may not limit an employee to FMLA's 12 weeks. Similarly, an employer may not force an eligible employee who is also disabled under the ADA to take an ADA accommodation in lieu of FMLA. Finally, just because a person is not eligible for FMLA leave because she has not worked long enough for a particular employer does not mean that she might not be entitled to leave under another law, such as the Pregnancy Disability Act.

It is a violation of the Act for an individual, whether an employer or not, to discriminate against an employee or prospective employee who requests or takes an FMLA leave. It also is a violation of FMLA to retaliate against anyone who opposes an unlawful practice under the Act. Employers may not manipulate job requirements to evade FMLA coverage, such as transferring an employee to another worksite to avoid the 50-worker threshold. Employees may not be made to waive or "trade off" FMLA rights. But note: if appropriate, and with full ADA protection, voluntary acceptance of light duty may be permitted at the end of a leave period under some state workers' compensation regulations.

HOW TO ENFORCE YOUR RIGHTS AGAINST EMPLOYMENT DISCRIMINATION

What should you do if you have been discriminated against on the job because of a disability? If you think you are being denied a job because of MS, you might discuss your complaint with the interviewer. If you are already employed, you might discuss it with your manager, your manager's superior, or the appropriate personnel representative, or go through an internal company grievance process if one exists. Obviously, this is not always feasible because of personalities, the particular organizational structure, or the nature of the complaint. You may think outside help is the only answer to the problem. How do you proceed? Although a full explanation of the issues involved in employment discrimination is beyond the scope of this book, the following discussion may provide basic guidelines (Table 3-1).

TABLE 3-1. COMPARISON OF THE ADA AND FMLA

ADA	FMLA
Employee entitled to reasonable accommodation for his own disability	Employee entitled to up to 12 weeks' unpaid leave in a 12-month period to care for his own or a family member's serious health condition
Part-time work may be a reasonable accommodation if no undue hardship to employer.	Part-time, intermittent, or reduced leave permitted if medically necessary
Employee may be assigned to alternate job only if unable to perform essential functions of regular job	Employee may be temporarily assigned to alternate job during FMLA leave for employer's convenience
Health insurance does not have to be offered in part-time accommodation if not provided to other part-time workers	Health insurance benefits must be maintained during leave under the same terms in effect before leave
Part-time work may be a permanent job accommodation	Employee must be reinstated to same or equivalent position at end of leave
Employee eligible for FMLA may not be forced to take "accommodation" under ADA in lieu of FMLA leave	Employee with disability who is also eligible for FMLA is entitled to the greater protection of both laws; e.g., maintenance of FMLA health benefits during part-time leave; reinstatement to same (not equivalent) job under ADA at end of leave
Employer may reassign worker to part-time or alternate work at end of FMLA only if that is a reasonable accommodation of employees' disability and there is no undue hardship.	

Title I

Title I of the ADA is enforced by the Equal Employment Opportunity Commission (EEOC) or designated state or local fair employment agencies. Local phone books should have listings to help guide you to the appropriate local EEOC office for filing a complaint, or call:

US Equal Employment Commission
1801 L, NW
Washington, DC 20507
(800) 669-4000 (voice); (800) 669-6820 (TYY)

Email: info@ask.eeoc.gov
www.eeoc.gov

Complaints must be filed with the EEOC within 180 days of the date of discrimination or within 300 days if filed with the designated state or local agency. The EEOC or other agency will investigate the complaint and, where appropriate, seek to resolve the dispute with an employer. It may pursue the matter by bringing suit against the employer. In any event, after the EEOC issues a "right-to-sue" letter, an individual is free to bring his own action against the employer. Remedies may include hiring, reinstatement, back pay, injunctions to stop discrimination, and mandating of reasonable accommodations. In addition to attorney's fees, a successful claimant may receive damages for actual losses, mental anguish, future losses, and punitive damages for malicious acts.

Rehabilitation Act

The standards for finding discrimination are the same under the Rehabilitation Act and the ADA, but complaints are handled by different agencies:

For federal workers:
The Equal Employment Opportunity Office for your agency (Section 501)

For employees of federal contractors:
Office of Federal Contract Compliance Programs
US Department of Labor,
200 Constitution Avenue, NW
Washington, DC 20210
(866) 4 - DOL (voice/relay)
(877) 889-5627 (TTY)

(Section 503)

For programs or activities receiving federal funds, complaints may be filed with the government agency involved or a person may bring a private lawsuit. For information on filing a complaint with an agency, contact:

Disability Rights Section, Civil Rights Division
US Department of Justice
950 Pennsylvania Avenue, NW
Washington, DC 20530

(800) 514-0301 (voice); (800) 514-0383 (TTY)

www.ada.gov

(202) 307-1198 (fax)

(Section 504)

You may seek the counsel of a private attorney at any point in the complaint process, whether on a state or federal level, and before, during, or after the filing of the complaint. Because there are technical considerations in deciding whether to file a state or federal complaint, you should consider talking to a lawyer before filing, preferably one who is experienced in employment matters. Neither the state nor the federal government will provide a lawyer, and if either of these governmental entities does sue the employer, it will be to uphold the statutes and not directly to represent you, although a solution to your particular grievance may be achieved.

A possible defense for the employer is the so-called "bona fide occupational qualification"; that is, if physical, mental, or emotional capabilities are found to be necessary to carry out the essential requirements of a job, an employer may exclude the disabled person whose disability cannot be readily accommodated. For example, a person who uses a wheelchair probably could be excluded from a job that required heavy lifting on a loading dock. But could a person with diabetes be excluded from a job as a computer programmer for reasons of physical limitation, especially if the disease is under control? Probably not. What about a blind person who wants to be considered for a job as a social worker but who needs a part-time reader? Some federal courts have held that in certain situations the expense of hiring a reader was a reasonable accommodation. However, the same or slightly different facts might lead to a different result in another court. This raises several more issues to consider. First, even if there is evidence of employment discrimination, the state or federal government may decide not to proceed with a suit. You may wish to sue, but that may not be practical for many reasons, including the cost of hiring an attorney. The prospective damages may not be enough to interest an attorney in taking the case on a contingency basis. The burden of discovery, hearings, and trial necessary to assert your rights may be more than you can handle physically and emotionally. It sometimes is possible to bring a class action or collective lawsuit by asserting that many similar individuals with common claims of employment discrimination against a particular employer should be permitted to sue as a group. This approach often has worked well in race and sex discrimination cases and, in some instances, may be appropriate for disability discrimination claims. However, the highly specific nature of each disabled person's claim may make it difficult to show that they belong to one group and have the kind of common problems that would allow them to bring suit together.

Another problem in successfully proving a claim of discrimination, particularly if the discrimination is suffered by someone already employed, is that an employer often may allege that there are reasons other than the disability for firing, transferring, or not promoting, and may be able to present evidence to that effect. In some states that have a strong tradition of "employment at will," anyone may be fired for almost any reason or for no reason at all, short of an employment contract or very clear proof of a forbidden form of discrimination.

For all its good intentions, the ADA has not proven to be as effective as its advocates had once hoped in saving the working careers of people with some disability but who believe themselves still able to work. This is true, both because of the technicalities of the law and it's application, and because of the realities of the workplace.

In practice, the ADA, as applied to workplace discrimination, requires the employee with MS, or any other disability, to walk a fine line between establishing "ability to work" and "disability" in the same lawsuit.

While some courts have certainly found that multiple sclerosis, and its symptoms, such as difficulty in walking, extreme fatigue, and so forth, can constitute "disability" under the ADA, the employee still has to prove that, despite these problems, she can still do her job based on some specified accommodation. In most of the litigated cases reviewed by the authors, the employee has not been able to meet this burden, either because the accommodation requested was not reasonable (for instance creating a new job, or allowing the employee to forgo job duties required of other employees); or because the employee's disability was so severe that the employer was allowed to conclude that the employee could not do the job even with the suggested accommodation.

In most cases, the courts seem to require only that the employer act "reasonably" in "interacting" with the employee and his health care provider on the ability/disability issues.

For example, in one case, a nurse became unable to lift patients because of her MS. The court decided that lifting was an essential part of her job and that the employer was not required to accommodate this limitation.

In other cases, where the employees complained that they were terminated or denied promotions because of their MS, federal courts ruled that the employees did not present sufficient evidence that their firing was based on discriminatory motives.

Furthermore, it is an unfortunate reality that when employers, and possibly co-workers, decide that they are uncomfortable with an MS person in the workplace, the practical problems of going in to work, even if the employee is successful in the courts, can lead to a great deal of stress and unpleasantness, which are difficult for anyone to sustain, and especially someone with MS, for whom stress and emotional strain may be an exacerbating factor for their condition.

For this reason, employees pursuing an ADA claim sometimes find that they have no alternative but to seek disability benefits before the lawsuit can be concluded. In some cases, the disability claim has been used against the employee by the former employer, who cites it as evidence that the employee was unable to do the job in question even with a "reasonable accommodation."

This does not mean that ADA protection for the employed person with MS is worthless. Whatever the likely outcome of a lawsuit, few employers are eager to be sued in federal court, since even a successful defense is likely to be quite expensive and, in some cases, injurious to workplace morale. It may still be worthwhile to pursue an ADA claim if the alternative is to give up a job which is highly important to you, both for financial and psychologic reasons.

Even if the claim results in only a temporary accommodation, it may enable you to extend your eligibility for various benefits, including medical insurance (see Chapter 5), and might help your claim for disability benefits if that becomes necessary (see Chapter 4).

As soon as possible after an alleged act of discrimination has occurred, discuss the merits of a claim, potential damages, procedures, claimant responsibilities, and other issues with a lawyer who is experienced in the field. You may decide to ignore the problem, to pursue the matter internally, to change jobs, to file a complaint, and/or to sue.

Enforcing Your Rights Under the FMLA

An employee may file a complaint for violation of the Act with any office of the Wage and Hour Division of the US Department of Labor. He also may file a private lawsuit. It is not necessary to first file a complaint in order to bring suit. Complaints or suits must be filed within 2 years of the alleged violation and within three years for a willful violation. If successful, an employee may receive wages, employment benefits, and other compensation. For more information or to file a complaint, contact:

US Department of Labor
Employment Standards Administration
Wage and Hour Division

There is no national office for filing complaints. Most large cities have Wage and Hour offices. For smaller towns and rural areas, call directory assistance for the Wage and Hour Division in the nearest metropolitan center. For general information and to request written materials, call: (866) 487-9243 (voice), (877) 889-5627 (TTY). For on-line information, contact: http://www.dol.gov.

In summary, you may expect your work life to be affected in various ways after being diagnosed with MS. This is especially true if symptoms are obvious or if performance capacities are affected. Despite inspiring stories in the media of people with MS who overcome all physical and mental adversity, for most people, some compromises will be necessary. Understanding what compromises or tradeoffs are needed and desirable in your work life is a vital part of your efforts to stay in control of your future.

4
Disability
Benefits*

Description of Social Security Disability Insurance*

MOST PEOPLE WHO ARE DIAGNOSED WITH MULTIPLE sclerosis (MS) have a strong desire to continue working for as long as possible. In Chapters 2 and 3, we have seen how the law can help (or, in some cases unfortunately, hinder) those desires. However, despite our best intentions, it is always possible that the time will come when a patient with MS will have to look at other possible sources of income. These include Social Security Disability Insurance (SSDI) and private or employer-provided disability benefits.

Anyone who has been diagnosed with MS should be aware of the disability benefits available from the Social Security Administration (SSA). You may hope you will never have to avail yourself of government assistance, or you may even harbor a hostility to the very idea of receiving benefits. It is nevertheless critical to know something about eligibility requirements as soon after diagnosis as possible. Federal programs such as SSDI, Supplemental Security Income (SSI), and Medicare/Medicaid (see Chapter 6) may become

---

* Please note that the description of the SSA programs, regulations, and forms were accurate at the time this book was written but is subject to change. You should contact the nearest SSA office by phone or letter for updated information, including pamphlets, copies of law changes, and other written materials. Also contact your elected officials. You may expect some delays in their fulfilling requests.

the ultimate safety net between the disabled person with MS and financial disaster. It also is of utmost importance to understand that you may take some actions immediately that will greatly enhance your chances of successfully obtaining such benefits at a future date should they be needed.

Like other SSA benefits (retirement, death benefits), SSDI is payable to workers, their dependents, and survivors based on the earnings record of the worker as measured in "quarters of coverage" or "credits." Some benefits are payable only if the worker has enough credits or, in the case of certain disabled recipients, meets other eligibility requirements.

The SSA keeps records of the amount of Social Security taxes paid by each worker. To find out how much in taxes and how many credits are listed in your account, visit a local SSA office for assistance or call or write to the SSA and request Form 7005 containing that information be mailed to you. When you receive the information regarding your account, check for discrepancies between what you think should be credited and what the SSA reports. Contact the SSA to resolve these differences. You must deal with this kind of problem within certain time limits as set forth in SSA regulations or the "missing" credits may be permanently lost.

Because many benefits are contingent on the worker/claimant first being determined by the SSA to be "insured," it is important to understand what is meant by a credit. For most employment before 1978, a worker received a credit for each $50 in wages he was paid in a calendar year. There are slightly different rules for people who are self-employed and for farm workers. Because of inflation, after 1978, the minimum amount of wages necessary to receive credit for a quarter of coverage was adjusted upward, with $1,000 of earnings per credit required as of 2007. A person may earn up to four credits per year. Therefore, if you worked in 2007 and earned at least $4,000 for the entire year, you would be entitled to four credits for that year.

Most benefits require a worker to be "fully insured." Forty quarters or credits of coverage (10 years of work) insures anyone for life, although more complex rules govern the relationship between the number of credits earned and the actual amount of benefits.

To receive SSDI, a worker must be "fully insured" (which may require 40 credits of work or less, depending on age at the time of disability) and have earned 20 credits in the 10-year period ending with the year in which disability began. Considering that this extensive work history would effectively eliminate many claimants with MS, there are exceptions to this "fully insured" requirement:

1. A person who is blind needs only 20 credits for her entire working life.

2. A person disabled before age 24 must have credit for only 1.5 years of work for the 3 years ending at the time disability begins.

3. A person disabled between ages 24 and 31 years must have credit for having worked half the time between age 21 and the beginning of disability.

4. Disabled children may receive benefits through an insured working parent past the usual cutoff age of 22 years if they were disabled before that age and remain disabled. This exception may be of great importance in MS if the onset of disability can be established to have occurred before age 22 years. However, note that benefits may be lost if the disabled "child" subsequently marries.

5. There is a special exception for a person disabled before age 31 years who subsequently recovers but then becomes disabled again at or after age 31. Such a person may qualify for benefits even if he has not worked long enough to meet the regular insured status requirement. This worker needs to work half the quarters after age 31 years to the quarter in which the new disability period begins, provided at least six credits have been earned before onset of the new disability period.

6. Divorced and surviving spouses may receive benefits at age 50 years if their disability began within 7 years of the working (ex)spouse's death. Also, the divorced spouse must have been married for at least 10 years.

7. If it appears that you do not have enough work credits to qualify for SSDI benefits, perhaps because you took time out for childrearing, for education, or to deal with your illness, you may want to consider ways to continue working, at least long enough to meet the disability requirements. This might involve continuing your present job or finding an alternate, for example, part-time work that will allow you to go on earning the relatively small amounts required to accrue coverage credits. In some situations, it may be possible to engage in self-employment, possibly in a home-based business or in conjunction with your spouse, so that you can acquire the needed credits as soon as possible. You must be sure to pay your self-employment taxes to receive the credits!

After a person's insured status is established, the problem of proving medical eligibility for benefits becomes paramount.

Obtaining Your Social Security Disability Insurance Benefits

So much has been written about the SSA, its solvency, its bureaucracy, and its regulations, that almost everyone must have strong opinions about some aspect of this subject. This certainly is true of many lawyers who practice in this area and who often are frustrated by protracted proceedings, inconsistent disability decisions, and fee delays. Some believe that as a result the SSA effectively works to restrict benefits, even for meritorious claims. The significance of this for the typical claimant is threefold:

1. The SSDI claims process, although technically an administrative proceeding, in fact has all the earmarks of an adversarial proceeding or a trial. A claimant must prove the claim and be ready, willing, and able to fight for benefits.

2. Although one should be polite and reasonably cooperative with the SSA, the claimant should neither downplay her limitations nor exaggerate her capacities in the application and appeal process because of a false belief that this will somehow favorably impress the SSA caseworker or encourage the SSA consultative doctors to file a sympathetic report.

3. If it is necessary to appeal a denial of benefits, the claimant should retain the services of an attorney who is experienced in SSDI cases, although this is not required. One may represent oneself or seek nonattorney advice and representation.

The first decision to be made about disability benefits is whether you are sure you need to stop working. Each person must evaluate his own condition in consultation with a doctor. Additionally, it might be a good idea to investigate alternative employment, including part-time work. You should think carefully about your work experience and qualifications, as well as about the limitations imposed on you because of MS. You also might talk to vocational counselors, teachers, and employment agencies to find out whether you can continue working, perhaps in a different kind of job. We say that this is a first step, but it is an important one, because once you have stopped working and have told present or prospective employers about your MS, you may not find it easy to get work (see Chapters 3 and 5).

To receive SSDI, you must first apply for it. This is done by visiting the nearest SSA office in person or requesting that an application be made by phone. In either case, a SSA caseworker will fill out part of the application. You fill in any missing information and sign the application. There is no particular advantage to visiting an SSA office in person. You also must furnish a W-2 tax form for the year before the onset of disability and a certified copy of your birth certificate, although the SSA will begin to process the claim before receiving these documents. If a claimant is physically or mentally unable to prepare and sign the application, a guardian or legal representative may sign it on his behalf.

The application must be filed while you are disabled or within 12 months after the month the disability ended or, in some cases, within 36 months of the end of the disability period. Because most people with MS presumably will be filing for a disability period with no foreseeable end, they should apply as soon as possible after onset of total disability.

To receive retroactive benefits (back benefits), a claimant must file a claim within 12 months of the month of eligibility. There is a 5-month waiting period from the date of disability (not the filing date) before a claimant is entitled to any benefits. Note that some people are successful in obtaining benefits by retroactively relating their claims to an earlier period of disability. It may be crucial in certain instances to be able to prove that disability occurred at some point in the past to overcome the burdens presented by the eligibility requirements for SSDI coverage.

WHAT IS MEANT BY DISABILITY?

Disability benefits as paid by the SSA are based on the concept of "total disability." There is no such thing in the Social Security scheme as "partial disability," at least in the sense that most people might think of this term. These concepts often lead to confusion on the part of claimants, their doctors, and even SSA employees. We discuss in some detail the technical requirements for "total disability," because proving your eligibility may sometimes be a tricky proposition. However, it is important to keep in mind that the concept of "total disability" in the context of Social Security does not necessarily mean that the MS patient must be confined to her bed or wheelchair or that she must be totally unable to function or to care for herself in her daily life.

Disability is defined in the SSA regulations as the "inability to engage in any substantial gainful activity by reason of a medically determinable physical impairment which can be expected to result in death or has lasted or can be expected to last for a continuous period of not less than 12 months" (20 C.F.R. 404.1505). The Social Security Act, under which disability and other benefits are paid, authorizes the Commissioner of the Social Security Administration to promulgate regulations for the administration of disability claims. These regulations, which are available to the public, appear at 20 C.F.R. 404.1501 to 1599 and Appendices 1 and 2 of Part 404 Supplement P in the Act. (Check a local law school, county, or city law library, the Internet at www.ssa.gov, or the SSA for specific sections of the Act.)

Appendixes 1 and 2, which often are simply referred to as the "Listings" and the "Grids," are keys to qualifying for benefits.

Basically, the Listings are a set of symptoms of various illnesses. With certain limitations, a claimant whose condition meets or equals the range of symptoms described for the illness he has been diagnosed with is automatically entitled to benefits. It is fair to say that the criteria for MS in the Listings are fairly restrictive. That is, a person may have a rather severe case of MS but will not meet the technical requirements of the Listings because her individual symptoms, looked at separately, may not reach the level of severity called for. The Grids are a method for determining disability based not only on the severity of the specific symptoms but also on the general ability of the claimant to work based on age, work experience, job skills, and the "residual functional capacity" that he may have to work after taking into account the symptoms that are present.

Let us first look at the Listings relevant to MS:

11.09 Multiple Sclerosis. With:

A. Disorganization of motor function as described in 11.04B; or

B. Visual or mental impairment as described under the criteria in 2.02, 2.03, 2.04, or 12.02.

C. Significant, reproducible fatigue of motor function with substantial muscle weakness on repetitive activity, demonstrated on physical examination, resulting from neurologic dysfunction in areas of the central nervous system known to be pathologically involved by the multiple sclerosis process.

11.04B Significant and persistent disorganization of motor function in two extremities, resulting in sustained disturbance of gross and dexterous movements, or gait and station (see 11.00C)

. . .

11.00C Persistent disorganization of motor function in the form of paresis or paralysis, tremor or other involuntary movements, ataxia and sensory disturbances (any or all of which may be due to cerebral, cerebellar, brain stem, spinal cord, or peripheral nerve dysfunction) which occur singly or in various combinations, frequently provides the sole or partial basis for decision in case of neurologic impairment. The assessment of impairment depends on the degree of interference with locomotion and/or interference with the use of fingers, hands, and arms.

. . .

11.00D In conditions which are episodic in character, such as multiple sclerosis or myasthenia gravis, consideration should be given to frequency and duration of exacerbations, length of remissions, and permanent residuals.

. . .

11.00E Multiple Sclerosis. The major criteria for evaluating impairment caused by multiple sclerosis are discussed in listing 11.09. Paragraph A provides criteria for evaluating disorganization of motor function and gives reference to 11.04B (11.04B then refers to 11.00C).

Paragraph B provides references to other listings for evaluating visual or mental impairments caused by multiple sclerosis. Paragraph C provides criteria for evaluating the impairment of individuals who do not have muscle weakness or other significant disorganization of motor function at rest, but who do develop muscle weakness on activity as a result of fatigue.

Use of the criteria in 11.09C is dependent on (1) documenting a diagnosis of multiple sclerosis, (2) obtaining a description of fatigue considered to be characteristic of multiple sclerosis, and (3) obtaining evidence that the system has actually become fatigued. The evaluation of the magnitude of the impairment must consider the degree of exercise and the severity of the resulting muscle weakness.

The criteria in 11.09C deals with motor abnormalities which occur on activity. If the disorganization of motor function is present at rest, paragraph A must be used, taking into account any further increase in muscle weakness resulting from activity. Sensory abnormalities may occur, particularly involving central visual acuity. The decrease in visual acuity may occur after brief attempts at activity involving near vision, such as reading. This decrease in visual acuity may not persist when the specific activity is terminated, as with rest, but is predictably reproduced with resumption of the activity. The impairment of central visual acuity in these cases should be evaluated under the criteria in listing 2.02, taking into account the fact that the decrease in visual acuity will wax and wane.

Clarification of the evidence regarding central nervous system dysfunction responsible for the symptoms may require supporting technical evidence of functional impairment such as evoked response tests during exercise.

12.02 Organic Mental Disorders: Psychological or behavioral abnormalities associated with a dysfunction of the brain. History and physical examination or laboratory tests demonstrate the presence of a specific organic factor judged to be etiologically related to the abnormal mental state and loss of previously acquired functional abilities.

The required level of severity for these disorders is met when the requirements in both A, B, or C are satisfied.

A. Demonstration of loss of specific cognitive abilities or affective changes and the medically documented persistence of at least one of the following:
1. Disorientation to time and place; or
2. Memory impairment, either short-term (inability to learn new information), intermediate, or long-term (inability to remember information that was known sometime in the past); or
3. Perceptual or thinking disturbances (e.g., hallucinations, delusions); or
4. Change in personality; or
5. Disturbance in mood; or
6. Emotional lability (e.g., explosive temper outbursts, sudden crying, etc.) and impairment in impulse control; or
7. Loss of measured intellectual ability of at least 15 I.Q. points from premorbid levels or overall impairment index clearly within the severely impaired range on neuropsychologic testing, e.g., the Luria-Nebraska, Halstead-Reitan, etc.; and

B. Resulting in at least two of the following:
1. Marked restriction of activities of daily living; or
2. Marked difficulties in maintaining social functioning; or
3. Deficiencies of concentration, persistence or pace resulting in frequent failure to complete tasks (in work settings or elsewhere); or
4. Repeated episodes of deterioration or decompensation in work or work-like settings which cause the individual to withdraw from that situation or to experience exacerbation of signs and symptoms (which may include deterioration of adaptive behaviors).

C. Medically documented history of a chronic organic mental disorder of at least 2 years' duration that has caused more than a minimal limitation of ability to do basic work activities, with symptoms or signs currently attenuated by medication or psychosocial support, and one of the following:
1. Repeated episodes of decompensation, each of extended duration; or
2. A residual disease process that has resulted in such marginal adjustment that even a minimal increase in mental demands or change in the environment would be predicted to cause the individual to decompensate; or
3. Current history of 1 or more years' inability to function outside a highly supportive living arrangement, with an indication of continued need for such an arrangement

2.02 Impairment of central visual acuity. Remaining vision in the better eye after best correction is 20/200 or less.

2.03 Contraction of the visual field in the better eye with:

A. The widest diameter subtending an angle around the point of fixation no greater than 20 degrees; or

B. A mean deviation of –22or worse, determined by automated static threshold perimetry as described in 2.00A6a (v); or

C. A visual field efficiency of 20 percent or less as determined by kinetic perimetry (…)

2.04 Loss of Visual Efficiency. Visual efficiency of better eye after best correction 20 percent or less.

Although these Listings appear to be very detailed and to incorporate some very specific language in attempting to describe the severity of symptoms, you may also see that there is a great deal of ambiguity in some of the terminology, with the use of words such as *significant* and *persistent* and phrases like *degree of interference* and *predictably reproduced*.

We may regard this kind of language as an effort to reconcile the very unpredictable and often subjective aspects of a disease such as MS with the need of bureaucrats to create at least the illusion of making objective decisions about individual cases. With MS (like most other medical conditions), it is impossible to look at a laboratory test or a radiograph and see disability in numeric or other unambiguous terms. If this were possible, it would make the jobs of administrators and judges easier. Unfortunately, nature is not that cooperative.

Before the addition in the mid-1980s of Sections 11.09C and 11.00E relating to fatigue, benefits often were initially denied unless you had the kind of extreme (and, in some objective way, measurable) visual and mental impairments not always experienced with MS or had motor deficiencies so severe that even SSA doctors would have to find disability. These changes, plus Section 11.00D, noted previously, have offered an alternative to the rigidity of the other medical requirements.

The other important part of the SSA regulations for the MS claimant is the so-called "Grids." The Grids are the categorization of claimants on the basis of age, education, work experience, and work ability. Unless a claimant is found to meet or equal the medical requirements of the Listings so that disability is virtually unquestionable, the SSA will make its determination based on the application of the formulas of the Grids. Although the Grids are controversial, their use by the SSA has essentially been upheld by the federal courts. What makes them particularly onerous, if not outright insidious, for the typical MS claimant who is young (under age 50), is well educated (high school diploma or above), and has a work history of white-collar jobs (classified as sedentary or light work) is that their use often will result in the automatic initial denial of benefits. This is so even if the claimant is medically disabled and perhaps effectively unemployable at a job with full benefits in the private sector by any employers who know of the existence of the disease and its effects.

The original purpose of the Grids was to help the SSA assess the trainability (transference of skills to a different but comparable job) of a claimant (often a manual laborer) who had been seriously injured. As a result, such factors as age, education, and work experience were considered of great importance, particularly when applied to the manual labor work force. But the SSA's use of the Grids does not always reflect the real employment problems faced by a worker with MS who has had to leave the job market because of this medical condition, voluntarily or otherwise.

Therefore, you should not try to be heroic when filling in the claim forms. You should emphasize your inability to work and not underplay your disability. Your claim probably will be denied if you indicate by your answers given on the forms that you can do sedentary work. Of course, it is extremely important that you tell the truth on all governmental forms and in any testimony.

Keep in mind that an initial denial of benefits or a denial through part of the appeal process does not mean that a person is not disabled. A denial is not always a true judgment of a claimant's medical condition and almost never of character. It often is simply very difficult to prove even the most deserving claim to the initial satisfaction of the SSA. However, many cases have been won by showing that a person's condition has progressed to the point where she cannot perform substantial gainful activity due, for example, to the fact that the exertion of walking, sitting, standing, or reading causes a deterioration of motor abilities, speech, vision, fatigue, memory, and so forth.

Please note that people have been successful in obtaining their benefits at a later stage of the appeals process even though they were denied these benefits earlier. Again, assistance by experienced attorneys during the appeal may enhance your chances of success.

Based on our discussion of these different standards for measuring disability, you may see that the decision to grant or deny benefits is bound to be, to some degree, subjective. That is, it is going to be based at least in part on the knowledge (or lack of knowledge), the prejudices, and the mood of the person making the decision. But this does not mean that the fact that a particular bureaucrat is having a bad day is going to permanently sabotage a valid claim for benefits.

If the claimant's application is denied, there are several levels of appeals within the SSA before the case may be taken to the federal courts. First, there is an administrative reconsideration of the denial by different individuals reviewing the file. Although new medical evidence may be submitted, you should realistically expect a result similar to the initial decision. Next, the claimant may appeal to an administrative law judge (ALJ), who will grant a hearing in person. A lawyer representing the claimant may present new medical reports as well as live witnesses. If the claimant is again denied benefits, there may be a reconsideration of the record by the Appeals Council of the Social Security Administration in Virginia. Only after these administrative review processes are completed may the claimant appeal to federal district court. Even then, the appeal is based on the written record and new evidence is not usually considered.

Although it is not always the case that an MS claim will initially be denied, it is true often enough that, to have a reasonable chance to receive benefits, you must be willing to persevere in your appeal. This raises several issues. If the claimant is not totally disabled from engaging in "substantial gainful activity," there is little point in applying and then appealing. A simple diagnosis of MS without accompanying physical and/or mental disability will not be sufficient for a person to qualify for benefits. If a person can work or plans to work part-time or earns more than the current SSA maximum amount of $900 a month (as of 1/1/07), he will not be considered to be disabled.

This does not necessarily mean that having a job automatically proves that you are not disabled. Many people with MS have been good and valued workers for years. Often after they are diagnosed and begin to have symptoms, their employers will continue to keep them on the payroll for quite a while even though their performance is declining sharply. They may be in what could be considered a "sheltered workplace," where their unsuccessful efforts to work may actually help prove they are disabled rather than the contrary. There also may be situations in which attempting to work in a new job that turns out to be unsuccessful may not be counted against you in proving disability, although you may not receive disability benefits for the period you were actually on the payroll.

As an applicant for disability, you may find yourself running into some of the problems discussed under the "fork in the road" analysis discussed earlier (see Chapter 2) when your disability claims seems to conflict with other choices you have made. For instance, filing a claim for employment discrimination under the Americans with Disabilities Act (ADA) might seem to be at odds with a claim of disability. The Supreme Court has ruled that filing a claim for Social Security benefits does not automatically bar a claimant from asserting an ADA claim because the two laws, ADA and Social Security disability eligibility, were created at different times and have different requirements. It should be noted that the Court did not say there could not be a conflict here, just that the claimant was entitled to the chance to explain and rebut the apparent conflict of interest at trial.

This case did not talk about unemployment benefits. There still may be a conflict of interest between claiming total disability for SSDI and claiming to be willing and able to work for unemployment benefit purposes.

A person may have representation by a lawyer or nonlawyer throughout the appeals process, with qualifications. All legal fees will be subject to SSA approval and generally are based on a percentage of back benefits owed to a claimant by the SSA. Many lawyers, even those who handle worker's compensation and personal injury matters, are not interested in SSDI cases because of the uncertainty of the fee, the slowness of payment by the SSA, a belief that there is little to be gained for the effort, and the opinion that SSA practice is unduly complicated. In fact, it is not unheard of for the SSA to pay lawyers many months after the successful claimant has started to receive benefits. Finding an experienced and competent lawyer in this field, therefore, may take some searching.

The application is rather detailed (see forms in the Appendix) and calls for a lot of seemingly innocuous information—hobbies, social activities, household duties, ability to sit, stand, lift, and so forth. Remember, these questions are there for a reason. Do not lie—the application is signed and a claimant is subject to criminal penalties for knowingly making false statements. Many claims are initially denied because the SSA has found reason to believe that the claimant is not totally disabled. So, although it is important to tell the truth, do not minimize your disability.

One of the most important factors in successfully making a claim is support from a claimant's treating physician. Not only must the physician believe that the claimant is medically disabled, but also she must be willing and able to strongly endorse the claim to the SSA. The doctor will be asked to file reports and send records to the SSA for review. She may also need to sign affidavits and/or appear as a witness at later hearings in order for the claimant to prevail. Doctors who have treated the claimant for the disabling condition and hospitals that have admitted the claimant for testing or treatment will be asked to submit forms and reports. Although some actions may be taken to clarify or correct an application in the appeals process—developing new medical evidence, challenging consultative opinions, bringing in lay and expert witnesses to establish character in work settings, vocational abilities, and employability—it will be much more difficult to win the benefits without strong and convincing evidence from the treating physician.

Besides obtaining a strong treating doctor, you may take several other actions to help your claim. One recommended by many attorneys who practice SSA law is that you keep a daily record of your physical condition and how it affects activities. Such a diary may be additional evidence of ongoing disability at a hearing or trial. And, as noted in Chapter 1, this diary also has the benefit of providing you with a record for future medical treatment and consultation with the doctor. You also should give some consideration to seeking out those friends, family members, co-workers, or supervisors who might be willing and able to offer evidence as to the effects of the disease on your life. Although this kind of evidence will not alone be the basis for establishing disability, it may help a judge understand your condition.

You also will need to show that you have cooperated with any vocational rehabilitation workers who have been involved in your case. The SSA may direct claimants for evaluation of vocational potential and job retraining by an appropriate state agency. Failure to participate in the evaluation/retraining process may result in termination of benefits by the SSA. Such referrals are not made in every case.

If required, the administrative appeals process may take many months; if an appeal through the federal courts is necessary, the case may take years to be resolved. Obviously, such an undertaking requires determination and discipline, which are difficult even for able-bodied people. Difficult and frustrating though such a process may be, it does not necessarily mean that you will lose benefits during this waiting period. If you are ultimately successful at some stage in the appeal process, you may be entitled to retroactive benefits beginning 5 months after the beginning of your disability (the "onset date"). This means that if you get approved several months, or even years after your application, you may be entitled to a substantial check for "back benefits." However, these benefits will not start more than 12 months before your application date. Therefore, as we said above, acting as soon as you are sure that you are unable to work can be important. If you are ultimately successful, you may anticipate periodic reviews of continuing disability by the SSA. For disability claims based on MS, reviews typically have occurred every 7 years, but this is always subject to change. Benefits may be lost if your condition improves, if certain remedial medical treatment is refused, or if you begin substantial gainful activity. The SSA regulations do encourage a benefit recipient to attempt to return to work by providing a 9-month trial work period during which time no benefits will be lost, including Medicare. However, you should confer with your lawyer regarding the possible ramifications of attempting such a trial period because successful completion may result in loss of benefits. Note again that, although Medicare may continue for many months after resumption of work and some allowances are made for easier resumption of monetary benefits if disability recurs after a return to work, this is by no means automatic.

SUPPLEMENTAL SECURITY INCOME

Unlike the insurance-based "regular" disability benefits (SSDI), Supplemental Security Income (SSI) does not require that a claimant have a certain number of credits. Rather, it is a form of federal/state welfare available to those claimants in financial need who meet fairly strict tests or formulas for individual and family income and resources (assets). You apply for it at the same time you apply for

SSDI, but it is approved separately, and in some cases, payments may start almost immediately. Payments may continue through any appeal process.

Several key points concerning this program are worth noting. Benefits under both SSDI and SSI are determined by fairly complicated formulas. However, it is generally the case that you would expect SSI payments to be substantially less than the SSDI payments you would receive if you have worked and earned the necessary credits to qualify. In 2007, for instance, the average SSDI payment for all disabled workers was estimated at $979 per month. For the same year, the payment standard for an individual on SSI was $623 per month.

A claimant may not receive both Temporary Assistance for Needy Families and SSI—you must elect which of the two benefits to receive. But you may receive both food stamps and SSI. As with SSDI, a recipient must accept vocational services, if offered, to continue to receive SSI. Although the disability standards are the same for SSDI and SSI, SSI is worth exploring with the SSA caseworker who takes the initial claims information, particularly if the claimant has minor children, does not have sufficient credits of coverage for SSDI, and/or has few resources, such as savings, stocks, or other property. In 2007, total resources of more than $2,000 for an individual or $3,000 for a couple (excluding many assets, such as a house in which the claimant lives, a burial policy, wedding rings, and so forth) would prevent a person from receiving SSI. Depending on the state where you live, there may also be a limitation based on your total household income from other sources, such as your spouse's income. The caseworker probably will be persistent in determining whether you should apply. You may receive both SSI and SSDI payments, but appeal of denial of benefits may be made separately.

People with MS sometimes are defensive and embarrassed about applying for Social Security benefits as a result of disability because they think that applying is akin to asking for a handout. Ironically, in some cases, these feelings have been exacerbated by expansion of the very laws that prohibit discrimination, such as the ADA, as well as the changing attitudes of the media and the public about the capabilities of people with disabilities. These changes are largely for the good, but they also may increase the psychologic pressures to try to soldier on even when the time to shift directions has arrived for both medical and financial reasons. People who have qualified for benefits by having earned the required credits should remember that SSDI is an insurance program into which their taxes and those of their employers have been paid during their working lives. Likewise, society has decided that, under certain circumstances, payments such as SSI are appropriate and desirable and monies have been set aside for such programs. No one should feel guilty about using the system for its intended purpose, which is to provide for those who can no longer work through no fault of their own.

EMPLOYER DISABILITY BENEFITS

Many employers, although a minority, maintain some kind of disability benefits. Typically, they are short-term and long-term insurance policies designed to pay a portion of the worker's base salary if she is disabled. Depending on the policy, perhaps 50 percent to 95 percent of base pay may be paid to the qualified worker who meets the standard of disability. The standard varies with the policy, as do the length of time the benefits will be paid and the percentage of base pay.

A key factor in obtaining disability benefits is the standard used to determine what is meant by *disability*. Some privately purchased policies and employer-provided policies have a standard similar to that of Social Security— total disability or the inability to engage in substantial gainful activity. Other policies are more liberal. They make some payments, at least for a certain period of time (often 2 years) if workers become disabled to the extent that they cannot engage in their regular jobs and/or have a reduced earning capacity.

Ideally, everyone would have purchased good private health and disability insurance before receiving a diagnosis of chronic illness and becoming disabled. Because this often is not the case, perhaps the next best thing is to find out the details of the employer-offered disability benefits available to you. Sometimes this information is routinely provided in employee manuals or employee briefings. Sometimes important information may be obtained from people who have applied for non–MS-related reasons; for example, a car accident, pregnancy, or heart attack. You may ask your supervisor or the personnel department directly. Of course, this may carry some risks. Keep in mind that, public relations notwithstanding, the managers and personnel staffs represent the employer, not you or your interests.

Remember, too, that the information you receive may not be completely accurate. Only the insurance policy itself, if there is an insurance company involved, governs the claim of disability. Most policies require that a person must be employed full-time when the claim is filed. If you think that the time has come to apply for benefits, speak to a personnel representative, your manager, and/or your union representative; ask to see a copy of any insurance policy and related employer policy statements; and follow the application procedures carefully. If possible, discuss the disability claim with your doctor before filing and make sure that you have his support and cooperation.

Be forewarned, however, that there may be a waiting period between the date of filing or date of disability (as provided in the policy) and the payment of benefits. There may be 30 days to 6 months or longer during which time no payment is received. There may be no gap in payment if the employer provides short-term disability benefits. However, only a few states actually require an employer to carry short-term disability coverage or its equivalent. Also, you may find that certain employer-provided health benefits will continue for a period of time after the onset of disability (see Chapter 5).

Be sure not to overlook alternative forms of short-term coverage that may be available to you at work, such as certain employee-pooled sick benefits or disability benefits. For example, some employers permit employees over time to voluntarily contribute sick days or vacation days to a pool from which they or other employees may draw income after they exhaust their standard allotment of paid leave benefits.

Many employer policies require disabled employees to apply for SSDI benefits if the disability is expected to last at least 12 months. Some policies may provide that benefits may be cut off if SSDI benefits are denied, even if the denial is being appealed. Because the standard of disability for the employer policy may differ from that of the SSA, you should talk to an attorney if you think the cutoff is unjustified. Some private policies provide for a trial work period during which time you may go back to work if you are in remission. Most will have a dollar-for-dollar or a partial reduction in benefits for all money earned by the disabled person. Most also will reduce benefits by any amount received from the SSA, including back benefits. Back benefits occur most frequently if an appeal delays the payment of SSDI benefits.

The insurance company or employer may periodically check on the disabled status of the insured. This may include a medical examination by insurance company doctors. It also may include drop-in home interviews with the insured, interviews with friends and neighbors about her activities, and private investigations into one's life and life-style. Because a great deal of money may be at stake over a 10-year, 20-year, or even 30-year period of disability (private policies usually stop paying at age 65), the insurance company stands to save a great deal if it can eliminate a claim.

It is the authors' opinion that insurance company review of claims has become more aggressive in recent years, including the use of private investigators. Although it is reasonable for them to review their claims, this does not mean that you should be subjected to intimidating, arbitrary impositions on your peace and quiet. If you think that their behavior is unwarranted, seek legal counsel, even if that results in refusing to let an investigator into your home. At the same time, recognize that engaging in certain behaviors or activities—rollerblading, ice skating, skiing, and the like—could conceivably raise a question about your underlying disability.

If the insurance company denies your benefits, or at a later time determines that you are no longer entitled to benefits, when you and your doctor think you are still disabled, you do have some right of appeal of this decision.

Unfortunately for many claimants, employer-provided disability benefits are regulated by the Employee Retirement Income Security Act (ERISA). This federal law was enacted during the 1970s with the original intent of protecting workers from having their benefits arbitrarily denied by employers, especially with regard to retirement pensions. Over the years, it has been applied to most other employee benefits, including disability insurance. Because of the way most disability policies are administered, that is by the insurance company which issues the policies, your main appeal is administratively to the insurance company. You may also have a right of appeal to a federal court if the insurance company acts arbitrarily or without any substantial evidence to deny your right to benefits. This can be a very difficult standard to meet. Accordingly, given the present state of the law, it is probably not wise to rely too heavily on employer-provided disability insurance unless your MS is extremely and inarguably severe.

Private Disability Insurance

The difficulties discussed above relating to appealing the denial of benefits for employer-provided disability insurance would likely be much less serious in dealing with a private disability policy which you purchased out of after-tax dollars prior to becoming disabled. Unfortunately, since you are reading this book, it is likely that you or someone in your family has already received a diagnosis of multiple sclerosis. Accordingly, because of insurance company policies, private disability insurance purchased after this point will either be unobtainable, or will likely be subject to a significant exclusionary period; meaning that you would not be able to collect benefits if you become disabled for some months, or even years, after your purchase of the policy.

Insurance laws governing these kinds of policies are subject to oversight by each state. You may obtain information about applicable regulations from your state board of insurance or commissioner of insurance.

5
Insurance
Issues

WHEN YOU WERE FIRST GIVEN THE DIAGNOSIS OF multiple sclerosis, once you recovered from the shock, the next thing you probably wanted to hear from your doctor was "What can you do about it?" The doctor most likely told you about the immediate use of medications to control your symptoms, such as prednisone or other steroids. He also may have talked about the possibility of affecting the overall course of the disease with newer drugs like interferon beta-1a (Avonex), interferon beta-1b (Betaseron), or glatiramer (Copaxone). He may even have told you about research being done in the long-term hope of curing or reversing the damage of MS through myelin regeneration or other laboratory approaches.

The doctor may not have spent much time talking about the costs of these present or future treatments. However, if you are like most people, after you adjusted to the diagnosis, you began to think about how you are going to pay for the care you need.

In the past, it was said that MS was not one of the most expensive diseases because treatments were relatively limited. This is less true today given the new costly drugs now available. Even if you are not a candidate for some of these newer drugs, expenses tend to mount.

You may be receiving long-term medications to deal with common symptoms such as muscle spasms or fatigue. Additionally, costs sometimes escalate when the basic symptoms of MS cause secondary problems. You may have falls or other accidents that need to be treated. You may develop infections that require expensive drug therapy or even hospitalization. You may need physical, occupational, or psychologic therapy to deal with the ongoing affects of the disease. Naturally, all these factors add to the medical bills.

In the United States today, medical care is built on the availability of health insurance for the majority of the population. Indeed, it is in large part the availability of insurance to so many people that allows, perhaps even causes, medical costs to rise so sharply for everyone. Therefore, being able to get health insurance becomes one of the crucial considerations in planning your future. Unfortunately, for people with MS and many other chronic illnesses, obtaining health insurance is similar to obtaining a bank loan—you can only get it when you do not need it.

In many states, at the present time, a person with a diagnosis of MS will find if difficult to obtain a new individual health insurance policy. If a policy is written, it often is exorbitant in price or seriously flawed in coverage. To many people, getting and keeping coverage becomes one of the main problems of the disease because in the absence of national comprehensive health care, a person's individual circumstances—where he lives, where he is employed at the time of diagnosis, alternative sources for coverage, disability status—figure into what may be available now or in the foreseeable future.

Fortunately, all is not bleak, no matter who you are or where you live. In the present piecemeal health care system, some people are in a better position than others to secure insurance, but some kind of coverage should be obtainable by everyone. Personal research or self-education is essential. Put another way, ignorance here is not bliss.

LEARNING WHERE YOU STAND

The first step in self-education is finding out your insurance status. If you are employed, what is your coverage and what are your benefits? Just as important, find out what is *not* covered. Collect and review your employee manuals, brochures, and other written materials that pertain to health coverage. If the insurance policy itself is necessary to answer your questions, get a copy of it. This may be easier said than done. Some "policies" are, in fact, self-insured benefit plans issued by an employer, which may or may not be administered by an outside company. You may be concerned about asking too many questions. Is this raising a red flag with the personnel department? Will someone become suspicious? This is possible, but if you have ever submitted a claim with your current or a former plan, the fact that you have the disease is available to the employer. Weigh the privacy concerns against the need to understand your coverage.

If you are not employed—if, for example, you are just out of school or have been out of the work force for some time—and you want to get insurance, how can you manage this after a diagnosis of MS? Again, individual circumstances may determine what kind of coverage you may expect to obtain through an individual policy. If you live in a state in where health maintenance organizations (HMOs), Blue Cross, or other carriers must offer an open enrollment period during which anyone with a preexisting condition may buy a policy, this could be your best way to get affordable comprehensive coverage. Likewise, associations—professional, academic, or social—may offer some kind of health care products (although perhaps not a major medical plan) to their members regardless of health status. Benefits, features, and costs must be carefully analyzed. For example, is there a waiting period on covering preexisting conditions? If all you can purchase is a hospital/surgical plan, what procedures does it pay for? Is there a cap on how much it will pay? If it does not offer all the benefits you may need, including doctor's visits, prescriptions, or physical therapy, is it worth the cost?

One method for researching insurance questions is to contact your state board of insurance, insurance commission, or similar government office. Be prepared for long waits on hold and often frustrating responses to even simple questions, but be patient; the written materials should provide a start for tracking down the kinds of insurance available in your state. State laws generally regulate what is called third-party health insurance, which is coverage offered by insurance companies. Many employer plans (sometimes called "self-insured" plans), which may be administered by insurance companies, are, in fact, regulated under the federal Employee Retirement Income Security Act (ERISA). This may sometimes create confusion for beneficiaries, so it is a good idea to determine what kind of coverage you really have through your job.

Laws That May Help

Once you have learned where you stand, you may still find that you do not have the coverage you need or that your insurer does not want to pay for the treatments your doctor advises. You usually have little control over what kind of policy has been negotiated between the employer and the insurance company or how the terms of the policy are interpreted by the insurance company. However, federal and state laws have been enacted to provide a basic safety net for people with health problems. These laws may be complicated and perhaps contradictory. The state insurance office should have publications that explain the interaction of various federal and state insurance regulations.

The Americans with Disabilities Act (ADA) requires that employees with disabilities be given equal access to health insurance and other benefits; their employment opportunities may not be limited on the basis of disability alone if the disability does not impose increased risks. However, the ADA does not prevent insurance companies from evaluating risks and setting prices much as they have always done, which may result in some limitations on coverage. An employer may still have preexisting condition clauses even if this adversely affects disabled employees. But such clauses and other conditions may not be used as a subterfuge to bypass the purposes of the ADA. Limitations on coverage must be applied equally. So, for example, an employer might limit coverage of experimental drugs, applied equally to all employees, disabled and nondisabled. However, if only those experimental drugs used for certain conditions such as hemophilia, AIDS, or MS are denied coverage, this may be discrimination.

If you are working for an employer who provides group insurance and subsequently lose your job, you may be able to continue insurance coverage, at least for a while. Under a law called the Consolidated Omnibus Budget Reconciliation Act of 1985, commonly referred to as COBRA, businesses with 20 or more employees must offer former workers continuation of health care coverage for up to 18 months, 36 months for spouses and dependents, and 29 months for people on Social Security Disability Insurance who are awaiting Medicare. This applies to workers who have quit, been laid off or fired (except for gross negligence), or had their hours reduced from full-time employment. Under the Health Insurance Portability and Accountability Act of 1996 (see folllowing section), qualified COBRA beneficiaries who become disabled in the first 60 days of COBRA coverage are also eligible for the 29 months of group benefits, as are their nondisabled dependents.

COBRA benefits may end earlier in some situations; for instance, when a beneficiary becomes eligible for other group coverage or for Medicare. However, this new group coverage may not exclude preexisting conditions.

You may have to pay the entire premium (the usual employee premium and the employer's contribution) plus a 2 percent administrative fee for COBRA coverage. This may increase even further for any time beyond the basic 18 months. It is critical to comply with all notice provisions and sign up timely for benefits, including any group-to-individual conversion options at the end of COBRA group coverage.

The Health Insurance Portability and Accountability Act of 1996 (HIPAA or the Kassebaum-Kennedy Act after its two key Senate sponsors) is an attempt to provide portability of health coverage to workers if they leave or change jobs. It applies to group insurance plans, whether third-party or employer self-insured.

Although the Kassebaum-Kennedy Act does not solve all the problems of uninsurability faced by people with a diagnosis of MS, it is an incremental step in expanding coverage options.

The law bars discrimination on the basis of health status or medical history. Employers, insurers, HMOs, and multiple employer welfare arrangements (MEWAs) must permit enrollment for all workers who are eligible for a particular plan at the same price irrespective of their health status or history.

It limits new-enrollee waiting periods or exclusions based on preexisting conditions to 12 months for any medical condition that was treated or diagnosed in the 6-month period before enrollment.

The concept of portability is related to limits on preexisting conditions. Workers who were covered at a prior job may become covered immediately at the new job if the employer provides group insurance. The 12-month waiting period is offset, month for month, by the period of continuous coverage in the old job. Continuous coverage means insurance coverage without a lapse of more than 63 days. An employer may still have a waiting period for benefits, including health insurance, but under HIPAA, if you worked at a job for 2 years and then move to a new job where your employer requires a 12-month waiting period, you should not have to wait for coverage because the time you worked at the old job counts in your favor at the new one. There are special enrollment rules for workers and dependents who have declined an employer group because they had other coverage available. If they lose the other coverage, they still have 30 days to sign up for the employer's plan. In this case, however, preexisting condition limitations may last up to 18 months.

What this means for people with MS who change jobs is that, assuming that they remain continuously covered, they will no longer have a period of vulnerability for health care costs. The concerns that resulted in "job lock," the reluctance to change jobs for fear of jeopardizing insurance status for the worker or dependent family members, have been lessened by the Kassebaum-Kennedy Act.

The Kassebaum-Kennedy Act also requires guaranteed availability and guaranteed renewability for small employers; that is, those businesses with from 2 to 50 workers. Insurance companies that sell policies to *any* small employers in a state generally must sell to *all* small employers in the state. They also must renew their policies. There are exceptions if the employee does not pay premiums or commits fraud. If an insurer can show that it does not have the resources, it may refuse to issue new policies, with some restrictions. The expected effect of these small employer reforms is to increase insurance options to businesses that in the past may have been effectively left out of the market because of cost and exclusions. Some states already had similar measures in place before passage of the Kassebaum-Kennedy Act, and some with more generous features. Here again, state insurance offices should be able to provide more information. The advantage to MS patients, particularly those who have or want to start a small business, is flexibility, although not necessarily at a low cost.

The Kassebaum-Kennedy Act also requires guaranteed availability of individual insurance policies. In general, a worker who leaves a group plan may not be denied coverage under an individual policy because of a preexisting condition such as MS. This does *not* mean that insurance companies must sell an individual policy to someone who does not have insurance. Insurers are required to sell only to individuals who have had 18 months of continuous coverage through a group plan, who are not eligible for other group health coverage, and who have exhausted any COBRA or other coverage.

States and insurance companies are allowed various ways to guarantee coverage, among them by providing high-risk health pools, designating open enrollment insurers (often a Blue Cross/Blue Shield plan), and offering limited policy choices. Coverage must be guaranteed renewable with certain exceptions previously mentioned. Insurance companies may discontinue coverage subject to notice requirements and limitations on their ability to sell any insurance in a state. Although the Kassebaum-Kennedy Act was passed into law in 1996, concerns about costs and the failure of some states to comply with all parts of the law have been widespread.

For more information and publications on COBRA and HIPAA, contact:

US Department of Labor
Employee Benefits Security Administration
Rm N-5623, 200 Constitution Avenue
Washington, DC 20210
(866) 444-3272 (voice); (877) 889-5627 (TYY)
www.dol.gov/dol/ebsa

Note: the US Public Health Service, Department of Health and Human Services, regulates COBRA for state and local workers; the federal government has its own plan with similar benefits.

How to Protect Yourself

1. If you are employed when you are diagnosed with MS and if your employer provides group insurance, you may have a powerful incentive for keeping that job even if economic or other circumstances might dictate a change. For example, if you were considering moving to a new job because of higher pay or for some other reason, look carefully at the medical coverage, if any, that may be available in the new job. The Kassebaum-Kennedy Act may help you here, but only if the "new" and "old" employers had comparable medical coverage. In certain situations, you may find that it is wise to keep a job, even if you are not completely happy, until you can find a safe place to land in terms of insurance protection.

2. Consider trying to obtain dependent coverage through a spouse's group, although more and more carriers are severely restricting the dependents they will cover. Sometimes group policies have a grace period, perhaps 30 days after the date of employment of the spouse, for dependent sign-up with no physicals or medical questionnaires required. See the preceding discussion on the Kassebaum-Kennedy Act for recent reforms in this area.

3. Investigate any professional and other organizations that you might join and from which you might obtain group coverage without having to submit to a questionnaire or physical examination. Even limited kinds of coverage that may be obtained through these organizations, for example, hospitalization policies, may be desirable in the absence of other alternatives.

4. In many states, there are open enrollment periods, perhaps a few days each year, during which a person may sign up for coverage at an HMO without a medical questionnaire or physical examination being required. This option is not available everywhere, but it is worth investigating with local HMOs, private insurance companies, and your state board of insurance or comparable state office.

5. Because there are risks of loss of coverage, plus possible civil and even criminal penalties for lying or deceiving an insurer about health history, you are well advised not to engage in this kind of conduct.

6. If possible, a person with MS should consider obtaining coverage by the methods suggested previously even if it means double coverage with your employer's group as a kind of back-up against loss of the employer group coverage. Note that insurance plans may have an arrangement for allocating "first pay" liability between insurers. In the case of Medicare, many individual or group plans will stop coverage after a person becomes eligible for Medicare. Also, Medicare will always look to a beneficiary's other coverage, if any (for example, medical benefits as a result of auto accident insurance), first to satisfy a claim.

7. Talk to your state and federal elected representatives to see if they can offer you any assistance in obtaining some kind of medical insurance coverage. Sometimes their influence may be helpful in these matters.

8. As discussed more fully elsewhere, Medicare offers coverage to those who qualify. If you become truly destitute, there are Medicaid and county and state medical assistance, which you may investigate with your welfare office or the county hospital.

9. Individuals with MS who have served in the military should check with the Department of Veterans Affairs (VA) to see if they are eligible for disability, health and life insurance, home modification, transportation, and other benefits. Certain health benefits may be provided free of charge to some veterans. Many requirements influence the granting of VA benefits, including the period served, length of service, percentage of disability, sources of income, discharge status, and date of onset, among others. However, the general rule regarding MS coverage for veterans who served during "time of war" is that they must show that they developed at least a 10 percent disability within 7 years of their date of separation (38 USC.A. 1112). The VA has the right to show evidence to dispute this claim. Other less liberal rules may apply to veterans' disabilities incurred in peacetime service.

The VA has formulas for calculating the percentage of disability present in veterans claiming to suffer from a condition such as MS. Veterans with dependents may be eligible for additional payments.

They may also be eligible for retraining benefits and a trial work period. Although the programs are not identical, veterans may apply for both Social Security and VA benefits. However, there may be some offsets of benefits. To obtain information on eligibility requirements and application procedures, veterans should contact the VA benefits office listed in the telephone book or on the Internet at http://www.va.gov.

10. You should consider contacting a good independent insurance agent soon after diagnosis to learn as much as possible about available coverage in your state. A process similar to the one taken to find a doctor or lawyer might be used—that is, talk with friends, family members, and referral services (see the telephone book, Internet, and/or contact your state insurance board for information). One hallmark of good independent agents is that they are more than "order takers." They should be willing and able to research the insurance possibilities and not just give a negative response to your questions.

11. You may want to investigate Medicare managed-care options and/or supplemental insurance. Fortunately, by federal law, Medicare supplements must now be standardized so that purchasers can more easily compare policies. However, not all plans are available in all states. Managed care plans for Medicare beneficiaries (the new Medicare Part C) also must be standardized. People should carefully study the risks and benefits of opting out of conventional Medicare before enrolling in a managed-care plan, including timing issues on starting and ending different coverage. In any case, it may be important to investigate Medicare supplements and managed care even before you qualify for Medicare because elimination periods for preexisting conditions and other issues may need to be considered.

12. Moving to another state that has more liberal insurance codes may be a feasible, albeit drastic, step for the person with family elsewhere and/or for someone who is not totally disabled but who needs to work and also needs the protection of good individual coverage.

DEALING WITH MANAGED CARE

In many states, more than 85 percent of people who receive health benefits through their employers are enrolled in some kind of managed-care plan. This is in marked contrast to the previous situation when most people with health coverage were in fee-for-service or indemnity insurance plans, which typically meant that a beneficiary paid for a portion of each expense, with a maximum out-of-pocket cap. The choice of doctor and hospital remained exclusively with the patient. In the two most common kinds of managed-care programs, HMOs and preferred provider organizations (PPOs), out-of-pocket fees are minimal but choice of health provider is limited unless the patient is willing to incur additional costs. PPOs are made up of doctors, dentists, hospitals, and other facilities that contract with insurance companies, employers, and other organizations to provide service to specific groups. They usually charge group members higher fees when they seek care outside the plan. HMOs designate physicians, hospitals, and other facilities to enrollees and typically do not pay for services received outside the HMO system.

Managed care has frequently posed problems for people with MS. This is especially true when gatekeeper doctors limit referrals to specialists such as neurologists. Similarly, there may be some difficulty in getting the managed care plan to pay the costs associated with visits to special MS clinics. The importance of a good professional relationship with a specialist with whom you feel comfortable, and in a setting that also meets those special needs for your care, cannot be minimized. If you are committed to a managed care program, there may come a time when you will have to consider paying additional medical costs out of pocket to hire doctors or to secure treatments that will not be covered through the managed care system. This may be not only because of your medical requirements but also because of other factors such as the need to have appropriate medical support in dealing with legal problems (see Chapter 1).

This is another instance in which it is critical to find out "where you stand" with your coverage because some managed care plans will not pay for referrals or other expenses from an out-of-network doctor, whether you pay his bill in full or not, even if he refers you back to a plan provider or facility for treatment. Likewise, you need to find out what requirements, if any, your state may impose for continuing care for the chronically ill in the event that an employer changes plans or a plan drops certain doctors. Keeping abreast of all this information certainly places a burden on the individual. Yet, the stakes are so high if you are uninformed that at present there is no good alternative to constant vigilance.

Like so much in our society, the confused patchwork of our health care and insurance system has grown based on all sorts of medical, political, and economic considerations. And, like so many other aspects of our law, we seem to have arrived where we are without ever knowing where we were going. You and your family now have a special interest in how the overall system functions. In addition to dealing with your own problems, you may be able to spare some time and energy to work with your friends and families to advocate for reforms to make these systems more understandable, less expensive, and more responsive to the needs of patients, especially those with chronic conditions.

Figures vary, but most estimates give the number of the uninsured in this country to be more than 40 million and rising despite continued political attention to the problem. At least there is some state and federal movement aimed at addressing this issue in general.

On the federal front, various proposals are in the legislative works. These include (1) the extension of Medicare to new populations; for example, the "near elderly" under age 65, and (2) legislation to encourage states to set up various mechanisms to cover those who are currently deemed uninsurable.

A few states have adopted some form of high-risk pool coverage. Although the premiums and deductibles are not low, these offerings seem to be within the reach of a financially prudent middle-class individual or family. A high-risk pool for health benefits is expensive to maintain and may, in fact, be a money loser to the insurance company participants. One idea in some of the state and federal proposals has been to offer tax and other incentives to participating companies. Indeed, the high-risk pool idea is not new in many states or in the insurance world itself. For example, high-risk pools are already in effect in some states for automobile, property loss, worker's compensation, and even medical malpractice liability. Certainly, these pools came about in large part as a result of group lobbying pressure. One would imagine that similar alternatives for providing health coverage, which could affect millions directly or indirectly in those states without such coverage, might be enacted as the result of vigorous individual and group lobbying efforts directed toward elected officials.

6
Medicare
and Medicaid

MEDICAL INSURANCE CAN BECOME PROBLEMATIC for people with multiple sclerosis (MS), particularly when their condition has reached the point where they are disabled from working. At this time, no comprehensive national health insurance covers everyone in the country regardless of age, income, or physical condition. Although recent federal legislation (see Chapter 5) requires states to provide some alternative coverage options to people with preexisting health conditions who change or leave group insurance plans, some states' alternatives are inadequate or too expensive for many people, especially those who are seeking individual coverage. Medicare and Medicaid often offer the only real alternatives to private individual or employer-furnished group policies. Medicare is to Social Security Disability Insurance (SSDI) what Medicaid is to Social Supplemental Insurance (SSI); for Medicaid, health coverage is based on financial need. In the past, the administration of Medicaid has been similar to that of Medicare, but both programs have undergone so much change in the past few years that what follows should be viewed only as an outline of the current system. As with SSDI and SSI, you should seek the most up-to-date information available about either Medicare or Medicaid.

The Medicare available to people with disabilities is the same coverage offered to people over age 65 years. However, Medicare coverage is available to people who are disabled for 24 months after they are entitled to receive SSDI. Put another way, because of the 5-month elimination period before you are entitled to receive SSDI, you may not get Medicare coverage for the first 29 months after onset of disability.

For many people, there is a serious gap in health insurance coverage from the time they leave their employer's group coverage and before they qualify for Medicare unless other insurance can be obtained. In the case of people with the very serious complication of renal damage or failure, the costs of kidney dialysis may be covered irrespective of disability status within 3 months of onset of kidney failure. This was a special exception in the Medicare regulations passed by Congress to address the problem of catastrophic costs that result from such treatment. For other disabling conditions, the concern about an insurance gap between the end of employment and the beginning of Medicare has been eased significantly by the enactment of the federal laws known as Consolidated Omnibus Reconciliation Act (COBRA) and the Kassebaum-Kennedy Act (see Chapter 5).

Medicare coverage is not always comparable to the best group policies, whether traditional fee-for-service or some forms of managed care such as an HMO. Medicare requires some coinsurance payment (partial payment by the patient for certain services). Low-income beneficiaries may be eligible for government help in covering premiums, deductibles, and co-payments. The hospital deductible, about which one hears so much in the television "Medigap" insurance advertisements, has risen regularly for almost 20 years. In 2007, it is $992 for a benefit period as defined under Medicare regulations. Unlike many group policies, which typically have annual deductible limitations, this benefit period deductible is not necessarily the total deductible payable by the patient in any 1 year.

A disabled beneficiary will be automatically enrolled in both Part A and Part B of Medicare, although she may opt out of Part B, which in 2007 cost $93.50 a month in premiums for individuals earning less than $80,000 per year ($160,000 for married couples).

Part A does not require any premium payments for most beneficiaries. Part A is what is usually referred to by insurance companies as major medical or hospitalization insurance; it also includes some home health services, which like much of the rest of Medicare have become subject to a great deal of controversy recently because of real or alleged cutbacks in benefits. Note: these home health services require a doctor-approved plan for care and may include various therapies—speech, physical, or occupational. They are *not* a form of unskilled or custodial care in lieu of a nursing home. Generally, entitlement to home health care under Medicare is based on a doctor's prescription following a period of hospitalization. Part A also includes services such as hospice care and psychiatric hospital and skilled nursing facility coverage. There also may be significant co-payments for care received beyond a limited number of days: 90 days in a hospital or 20 days in a skilled nursing facility. Under Medicaid (associated with SSI benefits), long-term or custodial care may be available if the patient meets the assets and income test referred to in Chapter 4.

Part B includes outpatient services such as doctor's office visits and medical testing. It has its own deductible (currently $131 a year) and co-payments, usually 20 percent of the approved costs with caps on what doctors who do not accept Medicare assignment may charge.

Medicare Part C offers standardized managed care options to all Medicare recipients. The same cautions that apply to choosing managed care in the private sector (see Chapter 5) apply to Medicare; chiefly, the need to consider the risks/benefits of limited physician and hospital selection versus reduced premium and co-payment costs.

PRESCRIPTION DRUG COVERAGE UNDER MEDICARE

Part D Prescription Drug Coverage, which went into effect in January, 2006, is the biggest change to Medicare since its creation in the 1960s. This new program will have some limitations for people who use expensive medications, like many MS patients. But for others who had no prescription drug coverage, Part D has been a significant benefit.

Fortunately, it is now much easier to analyze prescription drug plans than it was when Part D first went into effect. The easiest and quickest way to get information about Part D is to call Medicare at 1-800-Medicare (1-800-633-4227). Medicare's web site (www.Medicare.gov) gives the prescription drug plans available where you live. Click on "Compare Medicare prescription drug plans." Your state health insurance office can also provide information. You may also want to call you local National Multiple Sclerosis Society (NMSS) chapter for guidance. Many groups, including drugstores and insurance companies, among others, may have opinions about what you should do. It is important that you get all the facts you can and think carefully about what benefits are important to you and what financial resources you have. Even where you buy your medications may be a factor which influences what plan you decide to buy.

The big problem for many MS patients, especially those taking expensive drugs such as the ABCs (Avonex [interferon beta 1a], Betaseron [interferon beta 1b], and Copaxone [glatiramer]), Tysabri (natalizirmab), Provigil (modafinil), and Fosamax (alendronate) is that they quickly fall into the so-called "donut hole," or coverage gap, in a few months and receive no benefits for the rest of the calendar year. Although the Part D plans were intended to provide protection from catastrophic drug costs, it seemed almost meaningless if their coverage was to be exhausted in only a few months. In addition, some MS patients were shocked to find that the drug companies with some of the most expensive drugs like the ABCs, no longer provided free drugs to people who were eligible for Part D. All the companies maintain that they have analysts who will work with you to determine whether or not you get any financial assistance. Contact the drug companies directly for information. It is definitely worth pursuing these avenues for help along with some other resources for assistance.

The best-known medication resource for people who are uninsured or underinsured is NORD (National Organization for Rare Disorders, Inc.). NORD devotes a great deal of attention to the needs of MS patients, including some assistance for Tysabri. However, their resources are limited and a person seeking help from NORD needs to contact them as soon as possible for each calendar year. Their web site is www.raredisorders.org; phone at (203 744-0100, (800) 634-7207 and (800) 999-NORD (recorded message). Another possible source of assistance in handling high drug costs is the widely advertised Partnership for Prescription Assistance (PPA) run by the pharmaceutical industry. They will require an application containing information about your income and resources. Their phone number is 888-4PPPA-NOW; web site: pparx.org. If you contact Medicare and/or your state insurance office, be sure to research any assistance that may be available through them to help you purchase drugs.

Part D requires that beneficiaries pay up to $3,850 of their drug costs before they start to receive catastrophic coverage, meaning a small co-payment and/or coinsurance payment. You may need to consider purchasing a policy without a coverage gap. This will be more expensive, but it may be better suited to your needs. In any case, it is critically important to know what other drug coverage you may have from your former employer, a current employer, your spouse's employer, or your union since participation in Part D may cause you to jeopardize that coverage.

You can sign up for Part D from November 15 to December 31 of each calendar year without penalty, meaning you will pay the lowest monthly premium, but which rises for each month you delay. If you are disabled, you can sign up without a late enrollment penalty 3 months before and 3 months after your 25th month of disability. You should also be aware of other health benefits you may have, including COBRA, coverage from your last employer and all Medicare programs you may belong to like a Medigap policy and how it will be affected by enrollment in Part D. In some cases, you may not need additional drug coverage because you are already in a suitable plan. In others cases, you may want to buy additional coverage.

Participation in Part D is voluntary. This is also the case for any special Medicare programs like those under Part C (PPOs, HMOs). But in most situations, even those involving the original Medicare, a good deal of thought and research is desirable, along with consultation with knowledgeable and impartial third parties. Be sure you understand what you are buying from any of these plans, because you may not want or need all that some plans are selling. In some cases, the sales techniques are intensive. Get and read the literature carefully before signing up because the problems associated with changing can also be frustrating and expensive. Keep in mind that this is a new and controversial program. There is already a good deal of political pressure to change or eliminate Part D. Watch the news, contact your congressional officials, and express your opinions in regard to this program.

FINDING MORE HELP

As a starting point for Social Security and/or Medicare information call 800-833-4227 (voice); 877-486-2048 (TTY)

For Medicare hotline (beneficiaries' questions) call 800-638-MEDICARE (6833)

SSA Internet address: www.ssa.gov

Medicare Internet address: www.medicare.gov

Many consumer-friendly brochures on these and related topics, such as supplemental insurance policies or Social Security work, or rehabilitation programs, are available from the SSA. The usual warning applies: study everything carefully and seek informed counsel before taking any significant action.

In summary, bear in mind that all these government programs are based on an assumption of continuing disability. Disability may not be permanent for people with MS who are subject to remissions or improvements in symptoms. It may, in fact, be possible for them to resume rewarding, competitive, full-time or part-time employment. However, as noted previously, to avoid any undesired permanent loss of benefits, you should approach a decision to return to work with care, looking at both the medical and the financial ramifications.

7

Dealing
with Taxes

Taxes seem to be involved in almost every aspect of our lives. Therefore, it is not surprising that the person with MS will want to think carefully about the tax consequences of the changes that may occur in his financial situation.

What Is Your Income?

As long as you are working, earned income from your job will be taxed just as it always has been. If you begin to receive either a temporary or a permanent private disability pension, this will be taxable to you if the premiums for this disability insurance were paid by the employer, as usually is the case. They may not be taxable to you if you originally obtained the policy as an individual and if you paid the premiums yourself.

In some cases, you may also be eligible for a tax break on income from Social Security Disability payments if you have no other income. If you become qualified for Social Security disability payments (see Chapter 4), these payments will not be taxable unless you have income from some other source, such as a spouse's job or from investments that bring your total income to more than $25,000 per year per individual and more than $32,000 per married couple. If you exceed these limits, you will have to include one-half of your Social Security benefits in your taxable income. If your income from other sources plus one-half of your Social Security benefits puts you above the $34,000 income level ($44,000 for a married couple), you will have to include 85% of your Social Security benefits in income subject to tax.

Tax Savings on Medical Costs

Whether directly MS related or not, the costs of dealing with your medical problems may make you eligible for a tax deduction after your total medical expenses exceed 7.5 percent of your adjusted gross income. This is your total income less such deductions as contributions to an IRA or a Health Saving Account (see below), but before considering itemized deductions, such as your home mortgage or charitable contributions.

The practical effect of this limit, especially for the person with MS who is still working or who has a working spouse, may be that little or no deduction actually is taken because the deduction is based only on those costs over the threshold percentage that are not reimbursed by insurance. For example, if you and your spouse together have an income of $50,000 in a year, you could itemize only the portion of your medical bills above $3,750 that was not covered by insurance. Additionally, you get help on your tax bill only if your total itemized deductions are more than the standard deduction—including not only medical expenses over the 7.5 percent limit but also such things as interest and charitable contributions. In 2006,this base amount was $10,300 for a married couple.

Timing Your Deductions

There are several ways for many people to get some tax help by planning ahead. First, the limits just described are on an annual basis; you receive the deduction for the allowable medical expenses paid in a given year. Therefore, if you have any choice about when a bill is to be paid, you should try to pay it in a year when you will have enough medical costs or other itemized deductions that can be lumped together to get you over the minimums. This is especially important with doctor and hospital bills that you incur around the end of one year or the beginning of the next. Talk to your doctor or the business office of your hospital about scheduling your payments to give you the most tax benefit. Naturally, they will usually be happy to accommodate you if this means you need to pay them right away. However, they should not object too strenuously to waiting for payment for a short time, particularly if you discuss the timing issue with them before an expensive procedure or hospital visit.

You may have to pay tax in the following year when you receive a check from the insurance company if you paid a bill this year out of your own pocket to obtain a deduction. Also remember that "payment" means payment to the doctor or hospital. If you pay by credit card or borrow money from a bank or someone else to pay a large bill, you get the deduction in the year in which you pay the original bill, not when you pay off the balance to the credit card company or bank.

WHAT ARE MEDICAL EXPENSES?

In general, you may feel reasonably safe in claiming a deduction for any payments to a doctor or hospital for treatment of MS or most other medical problems. This includes any prescription drugs such as Avonex (interferon beta-1a), Betaseron (interferon beta-1b), and Copaxone (glatiramer). Remember that you can only deduct what you pay that is not reimbursed.

The key in most situations will be whether the money you are paying can be directly traced to needs created by your medical condition. The basic piece of evidence in many cases will be whether the treatment, medication, or other expenditure was prescribed or ordered by your doctor. Once again, you can see the importance of having a strongly supportive primary care physician or neurologist (see Chapter 1).

Some expenditures may be deductible even if not specifically prescribed by a doctor. For instance, bandages, crutches, thermometers, blood sugar test kits (for diabetes), and similar items are deductible if they are "for the diagnosis, cure, mitigation, treatment, or prevention of disease, or for the purpose of affecting any structure or function of the body."

However, the cost of special diets is deductible only if they are in addition to normal nutritional needs and not a replacement for them. Similarly, vitamins can be deductible if they are prescribed by a doctor as a treatment for a specific ailment, such as MS, but not if they are self-prescribed with the hope of improving general health.

Insurance premiums for medical insurance which you pay for yourself (with after-tax dollars) can be deductible. So can be premiums for long-term care insurance with certain restrictions based on the age of the person for whom the premiums are being paid. The younger the person, the less of a deduction you are allowed to take for insurance policies providing either nursing home or in home care. For instance, in 2006, if you were 40 years old or under, you could deduct $280 per year. For someone between the ages of 51 and 60 years, you could deduct $1,060.

You are entitled to a deduction for all reasonable costs of treating your condition, which may include more than just the direct payments to your doctor. You may also deduct the costs of going to the doctor. This includes taxi or bus fares or, if you use your own or your spouse's car, the reasonable operating costs, such as gas and oil; alternatively, you may take a straight mileage deduction of $0.18 per mile. If you must consult with a doctor in another city or be hospitalized out of town, this might include airfare, hotel room, and other travel costs. If someone else, like a spouse or paid caregiver, must travel with you to help you, their costs can also be deducted.

SOME "NONMEDICAL" MEDICAL DEDUCTIONS

If it becomes necessary for you to buy equipment or to make changes to your house or apartment to cope with your condition, you may be able to deduct their costs. This could be true of such things as crutches, a wheelchair, or a mobility scooter, as well as ramps or guardrails to assist you in getting around.

In the same way, if you are required to modify your car by adding a lift device or special ramp to allow you to get in and out, this cost should also be deductible when it is not reimbursed by insurance.

More expensive improvements also may be deductible, such as an elevator or swimming pool for physical therapy. In the case of major home improvements, you should talk to your doctor to ensure that she will back you up on the medical need for the expense. You also should be aware that the amount you may deduct will be reduced by any increase in the resale value of your home. You should not expect to deduct the cost of making the improvement look good, such as landscaping around a swimming pool or repainting the rest of your house after a modification has been made. To help back up your claim, you might get an appraiser or realtor to give you a written estimate of any increase in resale value. This often will not mean much reduction in your tax benefit because many modifications, including swimming pools, really do not add substantially to the resale value of the average home. Be aware that some courts have held that buying a house that already has a swimming pool does not allow you to take any deduction because the IRS claims that there was no expenditure in excess of the "market value" of the property.

As we said before, timing is important. This is especially true with the kinds of expenses just discussed because they usually may be done or paid for on a more flexible schedule than your regular doctor bills.

Further tax benefits might be available if you or your spouse is self-employed, perhaps in a family business. If you work out of your home or have to modify a vehicle that you use in business, you may be able to take advantage of the provisions of Sections 44 and 190 of the Internal Revenue Code. These provide for a tax deduction (thereby reducing your taxable income) or a tax credit (a direct reduction, dollar-for-dollar in your taxes). These sections might be significant if they apply because they may be taken without regard to whether you meet the itemized deduction limits for a particular year (i.e., the 7.5 percent of income limitation). This possibility might become especially important if you are trying to work in some form of self-employment to be able to qualify for Social Security Disability Insurance (see Chapter 4) or to meet the requirements for group insurance coverage (see Chapter 5).

Another area, which often is overlooked, is the cost of nursing care in your home. You may be entitled to deduct this care even if it is not provided by a full-time nurse. Maid service is not deductible, but if the same person who takes care of your house also provides nursing care to you, it is legitimate to deduct a portion of the cost.

As noted above, you can deduct for some long-term care through a long-term care insurance policy. This can include both assistance in a facility, such as a nursing home, as well as home care. To be eligible, you must meet several conditions, such as a chronic illness, like MS, which limits your ability to perform at least two activities of daily living for a period of at least 90 days without substantial assistance from some other individual. The activities of daily living referred to include such things as eating, going to the toilet, transferring, bathing, and dressing. "Substantial assistance" can include standby assistance from somebody else if there is a danger of your injuring yourself while trying to perform these activities.

HEALTH SAVINGS ACCOUNTS

You also might be entitled to a deduction for payments to a Health Savings Account (HSA), which is a plan that allows you to fund ahead of time medical costs you may have because you are covered by a high-deductible medical insurance plan at work ($1,050 annually for 2006). The money contributed can be used to pay qualified medical expenses, including premiums for long-term care and coverage. You can contribute up to the amount of the deductible under your employer's policy. One benefit of an HSA is that your contributions may be deductible even if you do not otherwise itemize your deductions.

Many people are concerned that taking large deductions, such as for medical care, will cause them to be audited or get into trouble with the Internal Revenue Service. An audit is always possible, although many professionals consider that medical expenses are not one of the most dangerous items because most taxpayers can back up their deductions with canceled checks and other proof. In the case of a particularly large or unusual deduction, you should talk to a certified public accountant, tax lawyer, or other professional about what you are entitled to claim and what kind of proof you should have. In any event, the purpose of our complicated tax system is to collect taxes from those who are able to pay and to give relief to those who have specific kinds of problems, including serious medical conditions. No one should be afraid to claim tax advantages that are in the law for his benefit.

8

Property, Powers, and Personal Choice

MOST PEOPLE WITH MULTIPLE SCLEROSIS (MS) WANT to be able to continue taking care of their own personal affairs and property for as long as possible. In many cases, your condition may be such that you can continue to do so without making any special legal provisions. However, you may need to make informal arrangements, such as letting people know in advance that you need to handle some transactions by mail, by computer links, or by telephone rather than in person.

Often, banks and other institutions will be cooperative if you explain what you want to do in advance. Messenger services, catalogues, the Internet, and other widely available services may be used to help you deal with business despite some limitations on your mobility.

POWERS OF ATTORNEY

If your condition has reached the point where you can no longer deal with legal documents because of vision problems or other limitations, you may designate someone to act for you in most normal situations through a *power of attorney*. This is a formal legal document that designates a friend, family member, or other person as your agent to take action on your behalf, such as signing documents or making decisions involving the spending of money or the buying or selling of property.

A power of attorney may be "general," which gives the other person wide authority to do things in your name. You should be very careful about giving anyone a general power of attorney, including a lawyer or a close family member. Even if you are absolutely confident of the loyalty of such a person, giving anyone that much discretion may be dangerous because his judgment about business matters may be different from yours. Even with the best of good faith, misunderstandings and hard feelings may arise, along with the loss of money or property. If you do need to give a general power of attorney, discuss it first with a lawyer or other disinterested party—not just with the person to whom you are about to transfer the power to regulate your affairs.

A *special power of attorney* authorizes the other person to take some particular action or to deal with a specific piece of business. You also should be careful to make a power of this sort as limited as possible so that neither the person who has the power nor the people she will be dealing with will be unclear about what you want done. This kind of power is commonly used in selling or buying a house or other property when one of the parties is unable to come to the closing.

Both kinds of powers of attorney often are given by people who do not have any kind of medical or other disability. As a result, you need to be careful in the wording of the power you sign because the law may cause a power of attorney to terminate automatically if you become disabled or legally incompetent, unless the power clearly says otherwise. Disability for this purpose means legal incapacity to handle your own affairs, not just a physical handicap. Also, remember that both kinds of powers of attorney may be revoked by you at any time, or given to some other person, unless they have language giving your agent an "interest," or partial ownership, in some part of the property or transaction he is to deal with, or otherwise satisfy the legal requirements for making a power irrevocable. *Only in the most extraordinary situation should you give anyone an irrevocable power of attorney over any of your property.*

MEDICAL DIRECTIVES

Often, the kinds of powers of attorney that people with medical problems are most interested in are those that deal specifically with health-care issues. These powers have names like *durable power of attorney for health care, health care proxy, advanced directive for health care,* or *medical directive.* The purpose is to appoint someone to make medical treatment decisions for you when you are unable to do so yourself. Numerous forms are available, many of which allow you to set forth particular treatment preferences for specific situations, such as refusing some kinds of surgery or procedures in certain cases. But because state law controls what is enforceable under these instruments, it is always advisable to seek advice from local legal counsel.

The same thing may be said for *living wills*, sometimes called *directives to physicians* or similar names.

The choices to be made in these situations are not always as simple as we might think.

We sometimes hear about dramatic cases, such as the Terry Schiavo case of a few years ago, and announce to ourselves and our friends that "we never want to be put on life support," or that we do not want to "be kept alive artificially."

Fortunately or unfortunately, there may be many levels of medical intervention between the point when a person is totally able to care for himself and the point when someone can push a button to terminate the life of someone in a persistent coma. These are not choices limited to (or even especially common for) people with MS, but are faced by patients and their families with many kinds of medical problems, such as strokes, auto accidents, and other chronic or traumatic situations.

State laws also control this type of document. These documents describe your wishes in the event that you are comatose and terminally ill. For example, you may decide to tell your doctor or family that you do not wish to be given food, water, or other medical intervention except for perhaps comfort care such as painkillers. These kinds of choices are often very difficult for the patient himself to decide, even when planning in advance, with a clear head, and with no outside pressure. It can be even more difficult for loved ones in an emergency situation.

For both kinds of documents, it is important not only to seek legal advice, but also to discuss your wishes with the other people involved, such as the designated agent and your physician, so that they clearly understand your desires. Even then, it sometimes happens that your wishes are not carried out for a variety of reasons: personal preferences of the doctor or agent, hospital practices, or just the general foul-ups that may occur in complicated situations such as a medical emergency.

Some states do have health care surrogate laws that set out a hierarchy of people—spouses, parents, or adult children—who may make treatment decisions for you if you are unable to do so. Clearly, however, thinking about your wishes in advance, designating an agent to carry them out, and discussing them with your doctor seems preferable to letting some other mechanism take over.

TRUSTS

If you think you soon will be unable to manage your property in general, in the sense of making basic decisions, you may choose to have a *trust* set up to provide you with a continuing income without your having to deal with the details of investing or managing your money. In this case, a trust agreement is drawn up by an attorney designating someone as the trustee whose job it becomes to make those decisions. You should determine that the person you choose as trustee is not only someone you can trust, whether it be a family member or an outsider, but also someone who is knowledgeable in dealing with money and making the kinds of decisions the trust calls for. A trust generally is created for a long period of time but, like the power of attorney, may be made revocable or irrevocable by you.

Along with powers of attorney, trusts may circumvent the need for court-appointed guardianships and conservatorships, which usually are more expensive and cumbersome. Certain trusts, sometimes called *supplemental needs trusts*, may protect assets while still allowing a person to maintain eligibility for government benefits such as Medicaid (see Chapter 6). Even people with very limited assets, who might otherwise believe that they do not have enough property to set up such a trust, may be able to do so by pooling their property with others. In such cases, they may still maintain their eligibility for benefits such as Medicaid long-term (nursing home) care. Some states have provisions in place to make this kind of trust creation easier to accomplish (see ARC in the Appendix). Trusts, estates, maintaining eligibility for government benefits, and related issues for the disabled are highly technical areas of the law that sometimes are even beyond the experience (and interest) of many purported specialists. See the Appendix for suggestions on finding lawyers and/or organizations that may have expertise in these matters.

LEGAL COMPETENCE

It is unfortunate, but true, that family members sometimes believe that sick people are unable to handle their own affairs. They may try to take control of property without getting permission through either a power of attorney or a trust because the patient is reluctant or unable to give consent. When there is a conflict between patient and family in such situations, resort to the courts sometimes is necessary. The family may ask a court to rule that the patient is incompetent. The patient may need to obtain legal help for self-protection and independence. In most states, to be declared legally incompetent requires more than a mere showing that a person sometimes reacts emotionally or exhibits poor judgment in financial matters. If this were the case, virtually everybody would be subject to a determination of incompetence at some point in their life. Just look at the behavior of the stock market on almost any day of the week! Legal incompetence usually requires that a person not be aware of what is going on around her, including the nature and extent of her property, and that she show a consistent pattern of irrational or self-destructive behavior.

This is another situation in which support of the doctor may be crucial. Most doctors do not believe that MS often leads to the kinds of mental problems that should limit the legal competence of patients, but symptoms in this area are subjective, and the experience of the doctor with these legal problems may be limited. Individuals who are concerned about this should find out what their doctor thinks about their medical condition from this point of view and be prepared to seek other medical advice if they are not satisfied.

WILLS

A person who is diagnosed with a serious disease will at some point think about what will happen to her property in the event of her own death or the death of her spouse. As you might expect, almost any lawyer will advise you to provide for this problem by making a will and updating it from time to time as family, financial, and medical conditions change. In a great many cases, the way your property will pass to your family at death will be about the same whether you have a will or not because state law usually says that in a typical family, when there is no will, most property goes to the spouse and children.

Even so, there is much to be said for going through the process of planning for an event that we all know is inevitable, whether MS is involved or not. In some cases, a will may reduce the costs of probating an estate and may make it faster and easier to sell property or take other actions after a death. People who have substantial property can save money on taxes. Most lawyers will tell you over the phone about their approximate fees for drawing up a simple will, and they also can also tell you whether you might benefit from a more complicated—and expensive—trust arrangement.

THE ULTIMATE CHOICE?

As shocked and dismayed as many people are upon learning of their MS diagnosis and its possible ramifications for all aspects of their lives, most people do make adjustments that allow them to achieve an acceptable quality of life. However, the media occasionally report instances of suicide—assisted or not—among the disabled. These reports sometimes include younger people who have conditions such as MS.

In February 1997, the National Multiple Sclerosis Society prepared a position statement on suicide and assisted suicide:

> For over 50 years the National Multiple Sclerosis Society has been dedicated to improving the quality of life for people with MS and their families. Suicide and assisted suicide are fundamentally inconsistent with this mission. We are deeply concerned about people with MS and their families and aware of how difficult life with MS can be. While MS is a chronic, incurable condition, it is not fatal. Depression may occur, but can be effectively treated. People with certain types of MS now have a choice of treatments that can slow the progression of the disease. Symptom management, assistive devices and support services also can enhance the quality of life for those who have MS.
>
> The National Multiple Sclerosis Society respects autonomy and the right to self-determination. We exist to affirm life and to offer programs and services that promote positive coping with multiple sclerosis.

At this time, assisted suicide is illegal everywhere in the United States except Oregon, and there it is subject to strict requirements. This issue remains an intensely emotional one for people of good will on both sides. Advocacy efforts, both pro and con, undoubtedly will continue for the foreseeable future. Any attempts either to ban assisted suicide or to expand its legal scope at the state or federal level will be widely reported.

9
Family Law

THE DISABILITY OF A SPOUSE MAY BRING WITH IT changes to the physical and financial aspects of marriage. Very often this creates a strain that is too great for the husband and wife to bear. When divorce becomes a possibility, the parties frequently find that the psychologic and economic burdens of the illness are aggravated by concerns about support, property division, and child custody. A basic understanding of the legal system that governs these matters may help both parties to cope with those questions.

The following are common examples of problems that might occur when a spouse has multiple sclerosis (MS).

A housewife has never worked, is disabled, then divorced, and has no Social Security benefits. Her husband promises to pay her so much each year as a settlement if she does not get a lawyer or give him any trouble. Then, a year or two later, he stops the support payments.

In another case, a man gets divorced, is assessed child support, becomes disabled, and can no longer pay the court-ordered amount. He does nothing and ends up cited for contempt of court and facing jail.

Even when there are deep conflicts between the husband and the wife, as there usually are when a relationship is breaking up, the marriage partners should try to plan their separation to avoid these kinds of situations, including the fair division of property and debts.

Unfortunately, the marriage partners usually find that the financial strains that often lead to the breakup of the marriage are exacerbated by it. This is because divorce leads inevitably to more expenses—separate living costs, legal fees, lost time from work—but rarely leads to increased family income. If one spouse requires personal care because of MS, the other spouse has often been providing. This obligation is another frequent cause of strain in the marriage. Yet, after a divorce or separation, the spouse with MS will usually still require at least as much care as he did before the breakup. This care must now be supplied by someone else, possibly a paid caretaker.

In almost every state, the basic requirements for obtaining a divorce are simpler than they were in past years. In most jurisdictions, no fault by either spouse is needed, and divorce is essentially unilateral; that is, one spouse may not prevent the other from filing and obtaining the divorce. The only questions are how much time and money will be spent fighting over property, debts, support, or child custody. It is common for one spouse to retain a lawyer and for the other to "waive" the right to appear in court. There is nothing wrong with this except when one spouse has more economic or psychologic power than the other and uses it to usurp the other's rights. Some divorcing spouses will submit to the wishes of their partner, thinking perhaps that there may be a reconciliation, that the other will behave fairly and decently, or that there is no alternative. This is unfortunate in any circumstances and may be disastrous when one partner faces ongoing medical bills, reduced income, and potential disability.

PROPERTY

Two basic systems govern the division of marital property in this country. The most widely followed is called *common law*. Traditionally, it provided that the ownership of marital property, both real estate and personal property, is to be determined by legal presumptions as to whether the spouses had made gifts to each other, had taken title in both names, or had advanced money from one to the other. Now, in most of states, legislation and court discretion regulate the division of property on divorce. In many states, fault or misconduct and the economic positions of the spouses may have a bearing on the division of property. However, the trend is toward an equal division of property irrespective of what either spouse may have done to bring about the end of the marriage.

The other system is *community property*. It is derived from the civil law of Spain and France. There are only a few community property states— California, Texas, Washington, New Mexico, Arizona, Louisiana, Nevada, and Idaho. Although there are significant differences among the domestic relations laws of these states, the concept of community in all of them, the "community" of the husband and wife jointly owns certain property acquired during the marriage. The property that each had before marriage, as well as some property acquired after marriage, is characterized as the separate property of each spouse. One spouse has rights to this type of property upon the death of the other, depending on such factors as, for example, whether there was a will, whether there were children of the marriage, and whether the property was real estate or personal property (money, cars, furniture, and the like).

In general, all property acquired during marriage in these states is community property, owned jointly by the community, that is, by both spouses, except that received by gift or inheritance or as damages for personal injuries suffered. However, the details of what is considered separate and what is considered community differs greatly from one community state to another. For example, in one state, income from separate property earned during marriage may be considered to be community property. This includes interest on bank accounts, money from the sale of crops, and stock dividends; whereas the sale of timber, stock splits, or births of farm animals may be considered separate income. State laws that govern the management of community property also vary greatly. The spouses may have joint management and control over community property, control only over their earnings and certain other revenue, or control over the running of a business under their management.

Property rights may become a thorny issue when spouses marry in a common-law state and then move to a community-property jurisdiction. Certain community states will treat property acquired elsewhere in different ways depending, for example, on whether divorce or inheritance is at issue. When the reverse occurs—a move from community to common law—the community/separate characterization rules may or may not be applied by the court on divorce. What the spouses expect from property division or alimony in their former home state may not come to pass when divorce occurs after a move.

Of course, in all too many cases today, the question of property division really ends up being a question of who gets awarded the debts of the marriage. Again, state law governs in most cases, and the result may depend on who contracted the debt, the purpose of the debt, and what property is pledged as security. In most cases, the judge will have great discretion in deciding which spouse must pay debts such as medical bills and insurance premiums, although recent changes to federal and many state laws make it easier for ex-spouses to maintain group health coverage after divorce, at least for a limited time (see Chapter 5).

CHILD CUSTODY AND SUPPORT

Although fault generally has no relevance in the granting of divorce, it may have a bearing in the awarding of alimony, child custody, support, and property. Therefore, the circumstances leading to the divorce should be brought to the attention of your attorney and thereafter to the court as appropriate. Similarly, the nature of the medical condition of the spouse with MS also should be considered by your attorney and the court in determining these matters. However, this may be a double-edged sword because there are cases in which the disease has been used against the MS spouse, particularly in child custody matters. But you should not let threats by a spouse deter you from retaining a lawyer and asserting your rights. The mere fact that a person has MS and may have physical, mental, or economic problems now or in the future will not in itself cause a judge to award custody to the other spouse. In almost all states, the standard for determining custody is "the best interests" of the child, although other factors such as the parents' or child's preferences may be important. This "best interests" standard may mean that a spouse will need help from an outsider, such as a psychologist or a social worker, including courtroom testimony, to establish the ability to care for the child. Here is another area where a competent and sympathetic treating doctor may be important. In some jurisdictions, the court will require a social study in contested custody matters that is done by a child welfare worker or other professional.

Nonpayment of child support may create a great burden on the spouse who has custody of the children, particularly when this parent is disabled and cannot work but still has the responsibility of taking care of the needs of the children. In recent years, state and federal governments have become more interested and aggressive in collecting child support payments from the noncustodial parent. The Uniform Reciprocal Enforcement and Support Act (URESA) has been adopted by all states and has simplified the out-of-state collection of child support. Likewise, federal legislation has been enacted that requires state welfare agencies administering temporary assistance to needy families to follow regulations concerning record-keeping, cross-referencing Social Security and Internal Revenue Service information, withholding of back support payments from welfare and tax refund checks, and seizing paychecks. As a result, delinquent parents in all states may have back child support payments subtracted from their paychecks. The delinquent spouse may even be jailed for failure to pay child support.

The Deadbeat Parents Punishment Act of 1998 (H.R. 3811) was a federal attempt to strengthen support collection efforts. It sets out felony violations for failure to pay legal child support for a child who lives in another state or for a parent who moves out of state to evade a support obligation. Penalties may include fines and imprisonment for up to 2 years.

Of course, the dollar amount of support will vary from one case to another. The noncustodial spouse will be required to pay some percentage or a fixed dollar amount of his or her salary for child support, depending on such factors as number of children and income. Federal legislation now requires states to establish guidelines for the courts to follow in setting awards. Despite this trend toward strengthening the collection process through uniformity of laws and active government participation, it still is fair to say that delinquent parents are numerous and that substantial delays in payment are common. Nevertheless, some of the financial and physical burdens of collecting have in theory and in practice been lessened, especially for poor or handicapped custodial parents. Therefore, it should not be necessary for a disabled spouse to accept the idea that he or she must relinquish custody because of a lesser financial ability to take care of the children.

Most people, especially taxpayers and custodial spouses, would agree that the new tougher laws concerning collection of child support payments are a giant step forward. Noncustodial parents might not concur. The noncustodial parents who have lost their means of support through no fault of their own—layoff, firing, disability—may in some circumstances have a good argument that their support obligation should be reduced. Court orders for support can and should be modified if financial circumstances change. Noncustodial parents should contact their lawyers and/or the court if they become unable to pay the amount ordered because of such a change in conditions rather than risk contempt of court and jail.

Relocating

A common concern of a spouse facing divorce at a time of limited physical mobility is the need to find a new place to live. When the move would place an undue burden on a spouse with a medical disability, this usually may be brought to the attention of the court and should be a factor in deciding who should move. It often is the practice of the divorce courts to allow the custodial spouse to reside in the family home until the minor children are out of the house. The value of the house may then be divided between the ex-spouses by court order through sale of the property. This may not always be practical financially and is at the discretion of the court.

ALIMONY

Although much has been said and written about alimony or postdivorce spousal support, the fact is that in most divorces alimony is no longer granted even though particular state laws may allow it. Typical factors that could have a bearing on whether alimony is granted and in what amount have been the economic circumstances of the spouses, special needs of one party, reasonable retraining expenses, fault in the divorce, and the general discretion of the judge. Alimony, although traditionally paid by the husband to the wife, may be assessed against a woman in most states and in some circumstances. Certainly, whenever special needs or problems are present—disability and ongoing medical expenses—requests for alimony should be seriously considered in settlement negotiations. Bear in mind, though, that any proposed property agreement or divorce decree awarding alimony should be carefully scrutinized before it is signed, because terms that were apparently agreed to verbally may not be fully reflected in writing. Here, again, the person without a lawyer is at a tremendous disadvantage.

Alimony may be terminated in many instances—for example, the death of the payer or the remarriage or even cohabitation of the recipient. In most cases, the court will have the discretion to modify the divorce decree or the alimony as circumstances change. However "permanent" the wording of the decree or settlement may be, and although of critical importance in some divorces, as a practical matter for the ex-spouse recipient, alimony will always retain a certain indefinite quality. Also, although there certainly are exceptions, many alimony awards are contractual in nature. If the paying spouse breaches the agreement, the recipient must usually bring suit to collect the money owed. This presents obvious problems in terms of expense, energy, and effort for a spouse who is incapacitated by chronic illness. Nevertheless, alimony may be an attractive alternative to simply dividing the marital property and debts in those cases in which there is little property at the time of divorce or if one spouse is expected to have high future earnings. Sometimes the use of alimony can be a helpful tax-planning device, since it is generally deductible against the income of the spouse who pays it and taxable to the spouse who receives it. This can be especially useful when there is a considerable disparity between the incomes (and therefore the tax bill) of the two spouses.

Under the revised bankruptcy law (see Chapter 10), child and spousal support obligations are generally not dischargeable in bankruptcy, and these marital obligations have a high priority claim on the assets of a debtor.

Related to this question of mutual support obligations is the issue of rights under pensions and other entitlements, which may be "property" subject to division or award on divorce. State and federal laws vary widely. For example, certain government pensions may be considered divisible in whole or in part in some circumstances. In some states, marital property may include disability pay, professional licenses, professional practices or businesses, and worker's compensation. Because of the complexity of the issues involved in determining if or how some of these sources of income may be affected by divorce under the laws of a particular jurisdiction, a divorcing spouse, especially one whose future is clouded by a medical condition such as MS, should make sure that his rights are protected fully.

It is tragic that all too often the spouse with MS does not look after his rights. This may be due not only to ignorance but also to guilt feelings—the tendency to think, consciously or unconsciously, that the marital problems are "all my fault" for having the disease in the first place. These feelings often exact an unnecessarily high price from the individual with MS and may result in even greater resentment and hostility by the other spouse. In any event, the least any marriage partner should try to salvage from a failing relationship is financial survival and emotional self-respect. The law can help to achieve this for both spouses.

10
Handling Your Debts

THE ISSUES OF DEBTOR/CREDITOR RIGHTS LOOM LARGE if you have lost your job and income, are faced with rising medical costs, have been deserted by a spouse and left with minor children, or are receiving collection letters and dunning calls.

Our purpose is not to suggest that anyone should avoid paying lawful debts. Despite the advice of some popular financial advisors, you should avoid burdensome debt and try to live within your means. But disasters such as disabling illness do strike and may cancel previously sound financial plans. What follows is a very brief discussion of a few key state and federal statutes as they relate to debt problems.

If you have a delinquent debt, whether due to sudden medical costs not covered by insurance, loss of a job, or any other reason, the best advice is do not panic. Although there are important practical and moral reasons for wanting to pay your bills on time, failure to do so normally is not a crime. Some medical authorities say that there is a personality type often associated with multiple sclerosis (MS) that is characterized by an overdeveloped sense of responsibility. When you are in a strained financial condition, this sense of responsibility should show itself by your trying to work with your existing resources to make the best arrangements you can, including paying your debts, while still allowing yourself a decent standard of living.

The first step is to make a budget to give yourself a realistic view of how much you have coming in and what you must spend to make rent or house payments, buy groceries, and pay for other necessities. The amount you have left may then be used to make payments on existing debts. If this amount is not enough to make the scheduled payments in full, you may want to talk to your creditors and ask them to agree to take smaller payments over a longer period of time. Sometimes creditors will be more willing than you might expect to make this type of arrangement because they have enough experience with people in financial trouble to know that the alternatives may be worse from their point of view, as well as from yours. If your debts are large and complicated, you might need to talk to a lawyer or debt counselor about getting help in drawing up a plan of this kind; often called a creditor's arrangement.

If a creditor is not willing to work things out with you or if your circumstances reach the point where you are unable to make even token payments, the creditor may take you to court by filing suit for debt. If the debt is *secured*, that is, if some property, such as a car or your house, is pledged as collateral, the creditor may seek to foreclose and take back the property. If you have some basis to dispute the claim or believe that you do not owe the full amount a creditor is asking for, you may hire a lawyer and require the creditor to prove the case to a judge or jury. You are not *required* to have a lawyer, but you will be at a tremendous disadvantage without one. If you lose, you may expect to owe a judgment for the amount of the debt plus the creditor's court costs and, in some states, legal fees.

Even if a creditor takes a judgment against you, it does not necessarily mean that you are ruined or that you will lose everything you have. Some states give more protection to debtors in this situation than others. In no state may creditors with a judgment have you put in jail (with a limited exception for parents who owe child support and refuse to pay), but they may take certain other actions to collect, some of which are outlined here.

Garnishment

Garnishment refers to the legal procedure whereby a debtor's property that is in the hands of a third party is taken by a creditor to satisfy a preexisting debt, usually after a court judgment. Most often the property in question is held by an employer (paychecks) or a bank (bank accounts).

Most states allow garnishment of wages for debts, but there are limits on the total amount of "disposable wages" that may be taken by creditors. Under the federal Consumer Protection Act, only 25 percent of disposable wages, defined as salary minus all deductions required by law, such as taxes and Social Security, may be garnished. There are differences in state laws as to what property is subject to garnishment. It is important to keep in mind, though, that many creditors will try to garnish wages for relatively small debts. Therefore, if you receive notice of an intention to garnish wages or attach (to take or seize) property, contact the creditor and/or a lawyer immediately to try to resolve the problem. If the creditor is unwilling to work with you, or if the amount of the debts involved is too large, you may need to consider some form of bankruptcy protection, as discussed below. Some income, such as certain disability income, may not be used by creditors to satisfy most debts. Again, you must discuss this point with a lawyer in your state to determine whether this or any other income or property will be outside the reach of your creditors.

EXECUTION

The creditor may have the judgment given to the sheriff or constable to take property of the debtor, which then is sold to pay the debt. All states exempt certain property from seizure by creditors to satisfy debts. The types and amount of property exempt from seizure vary significantly from state to state. Often this is the *real property*—the home, frequently referred to as the "homestead," where the debtor and his family live. Sometimes specific property—a car, tools, life insurance, personal effects, food, pets—is protected from seizure. Sometimes property up to a certain dollar value is exempt.

What this all means, in brief, is that creditors may not seize exempt property of the debtor to satisfy debts. For example, although a hospital may sue you for nonpayment of a bill and obtain a judgment against you, it may not be able to take your house, car, household goods, and so forth, to satisfy the judgment. In many states, however, it may be able to get a lien that may limit your right to sell the property without first satisfying the debt. A judgment may be in effect for a number of years. If you acquire nonexempt property while the judgment is in effect, the creditor with the judgment may be able to seize it.

There are some significant exceptions to the exempt property protections just described. The Internal Revenue Service may seize almost any property to satisfy a tax debt. Creditors who lent you the money to buy property, such as a car, may seize or foreclose on the collateral; for example, the finance company may repossess the car for which it lent money to you. The mortgage company may foreclose on the real estate, lot, and improvements it helped you to buy even if it is designated a homestead. Contractors may obtain a lien on real property for improvements they have made (swimming pool, roof, plumbing) and also may, with some restrictions, take back the improvements. In many states, most of the property of a debtor may be pledged or "put up" to secure loans, although in some states, certain exemptions may still apply to such property in narrowly prescribed circumstances.

State and local governmental entities may also get judgments against a person who owes taxes and fees, and may take homestead property to satisfy such debts.

BANKRUPTCY

When debt problems threaten to become overwhelming, the debtor may need to take advantage of the protection of the federal bankruptcy laws by filing for bankruptcy under Chapter 7 or Chapter 13 of the United States Bankruptcy Code. This is one of the many areas discussed in this book in which you are well advised to consult a knowledgeable and experienced lawyer. This is particularly true in light of revisions to the bankruptcy laws which went into effect in October 2005.

Prior to seeking protection from the bankruptcy court, a debtor is now required in most situations to obtain credit counseling from an agency licensed by the United States Bankruptcy Court for the district in which he lives. This counseling session, which is usually conducted by telephone or by an online conference, will require that you tell the credit counseling agency details of your financial problems and the reason why you think you need the bankruptcy protection. The credit counseling agency is then required to give you a written certificate acknowledging that you have had the counseling session and are eligible to seek relief. This certificate must be filed with the first papers in your bankruptcy case.

A debtor may file a *straight* bankruptcy, or a *Chapter 7*, which is a liquidation of assets. In this action, you may keep certain exempt property, but must give up other assets. The proceeds will be paid to creditors under the direction of a bankruptcy court. Most debts can be discharged or wiped out in a Chapter 7 bankruptcy. One common reason for choosing a Chapter 7 bankruptcy is the amount of the unsecured debts which are debts for which there is no collateral, such as a house or car. These may include large medical or credit card bills and even (in limited situations) income taxes for prior years.

The other alternative, a wage-earner plan, or a Chapter 13, is a way of paying some or all of your debts over a period of time, up to 5 years. This is usually resorted to when you have gotten behind on secured debts, such as a home mortgage or a car payment, or if you owe taxes which cannot be forgiven in a Chapter 7 bankruptcy.

Changes in the bankruptcy law in 2006 create guidelines which may require debtors to choose Chapter 13, rather than Chapter 7, if their household income is above average for the state where they live.

There are several eligibility requirements for filing a Chapter 13, chief among them that the debtor be an individual with regular income so that he will be able to make stable and regular payments under a repayment plan. By this definition, even an individual operating a small business or a person receiving disability income, welfare, or other "nonwage" income may qualify. Spouses may file separately or jointly. There also is a debt ceiling for people who file a Chapter 13 bankruptcy. For an individual or spouses filing jointly, the unsecured debt (no collateral) total may not exceed $303,000; the secured debt (collateral) may not exceed $1,000,000.

Other important features of a Chapter 13 bankruptcy include the following:

1. The debtor is protected, with some qualifications, from collection efforts of creditors while the plan of repayment is in effect.

2. The debtor submits a part of future income to the bankruptcy trustee as part of a repayment plan approved by the bankruptcy court.

3. In some circumstances, a creditor may object to a plan if she thinks you can pay off your debts faster than the plan provides for.

4. Although some plans provide for 100 percent repayment of creditors, many plans do not. There often is a guideline percentage that the court follows in approving plans, but even here there is considerable variation based on the financial situation of each debtor. At the end of the plan, the debtor will be discharged (released) from most debts.

Certain debts, including alimony, maintenance, child support, and most taxes, are not dischargeable or wiped out by bankruptcy, although under a Chapter 13 plan, they may be paid over an extended period. Debts that are *unscheduled*, that is, are not listed in the bankruptcy papers, or that arose through conscious "bad acts" such as fraud or willful conduct, may also be nondischargeable.

Many people are concerned about filing bankruptcy because of the psychologic stigma or the expected effect on future credit. These are reasonable concerns. However, people who later get themselves on a stronger financial footing usually can obtain credit when they need it. Bankruptcy rarely is worse for your credit history than a constant barrage of collection efforts by unpaid creditors. The purpose of the bankruptcy statutes is to allow people to rebuild their financial lives. No one should feel ashamed as long as he is undertaking this action in good faith and after exhausting other efforts to pay his bills.

PROTECTION FROM BILL COLLECTIONS

Filing bankruptcy automatically stops collection activity by creditors except through the bankruptcy court. Even short of filing for bankruptcy, there are protections for the debtor from extreme harassment by creditors. Debt collection practices are regulated by both federal and state laws, principally the federal Fair Debt Collection Practices Act and individual state statutes. The state acts typically apply to consumer debts, as does the federal law. The federal Act regulates collection agents and their practices. There also are common law tort theories relating to privacy, defamation, and infliction of mental distress that may apply to unfair collection practices.

Among the most significant unlawful debt collection practices under these statutes are threats of criminal action if the debt is not paid, calling employers and discussing the debtor's debt with them, phoning or visiting the debtor early in the morning or late in the evening, making abusive, harassing calls to the debtor or the debtor's family, and continuing to harass the debtor personally after the creditor or agent has been advised that a debt is in dispute.

The Acts noted provide penalties for violators, including costs, attorney's fees, and, in some cases, cancellation of the debt.

11
Getting Around
with Multiple Sclerosis

W E LIVE IN A WORLD THAT IS INCREASINGLY CROWDED and stressful. Sad to say, the inevitable friction of life in trying to get from point A to point B is aggravated when we suffer from some degree of physical disability. There may be frustrating obstacles in our efforts to travel, use public accommodations, and even find a place to live.

This chapter discusses how the law may help you to deal with some of these obstacles and to make daily life a little more user-friendly.

FLYING WITH MULTIPLE SCLEROSIS

Traveling by air seems to become more difficult each year. There are more packed airports, with gates farther apart, giving access to fewer and less competitive airlines, which put you on planes with smaller seats and more limited luggage space. In the wake of the September 11, 2001, terrorist attacks, these problems have been exacerbated by the delays and inconvenience inevitable with the higher level of airport security. Because of the reduced number of flights and the frequent overbooking of the seats available, being late for a flight can result in long delays. If you are less than an Olympic athlete in terms of getting on and off the plane, you may think a little extra consideration on the part of the airlines and their employees would be welcome. The law gives you some back-up on this point.

The Air Carrier Access Act of 1986 (the Act) (49 USC 1374[(c)]) prohibits discrimination against people with disabilities in flying. A qualified individual with a disability must be allowed the same rights and opportunities as the rest of the flying public, with due regard for safety and economic factors. Where this law has made the most difference for many people with impaired mobility is in regulating how passengers who use wheelchairs, motorized scooters, and other devices are to be treated by the airlines. In conjunction with other laws, the Air Carrier Access Act also requires that airport parking, ground transportation, terminals, and gateways be accessible, with a phase-in over several years for small nonhub airports.

Airplane accessibility itself and on-board availability and storage of mobility devices such as folding wheelchairs are determined by plane size. Planes with 30 or more passenger seats must have movable armrests on at least half the aisle seats. Planes with 100 or more seats must provide cabin storage space for at least one folding wheelchair. Aircraft with more than one aisle must have a wheelchair-accessible lavatory. If a passenger can use an inaccessible lavatory with the help of an on-board wheelchair, planes with 60 seats must make a chair available when the passenger gives advance notice (up to 48 hours). New planes delivered after April 1992 must meet these standards; older planes must come into compliance as they are refurbished, making full accessibility a phased-in process.

In general, medium and large planes (those with more than 30 seats) must be boardable by ramp or lift. This does not mean the lift used for freight! Airline personnel are required to take training to help them assist passengers with disabilities, and although they are not required to offer personal care assistance such as feeding, lifting, or providing medical services, they often do assist with transfers.

Accessibility remains a problem with smaller commuter planes and airports because some small planes and airports are exempt from the Act either permanently or for a number of years to come. However, the major airlines and their commuter lines are for the most part accessible.

Your legal protections do not stop when you reach the ground. Because of interconnected provisions of the Rehabilitation Act of 1973, the Air Carrier Act, and the Americans with Disabilities Act (ADA), you have a right to accessibility of buildings, ramps, curbs, restrooms, parking, and other facilities at airports and related installations. Based on regulations issued in early 1998, it appears that people with multiple sclerosis (MS) and other disabilities may ask that appropriate provisions of these laws be applied as needed to ensure fair access to aircraft and airports.

Here are some tips that may be useful for dealing with the airlines:

1. A disabled passenger does not *have* to give a carrier any advance notice of his condition except in certain limited circumstances, such as the request for an on-board wheelchair for a plane that does not have an accessible lavatory, but the airline's duty to accommodate you may be lessened if you do not. As a practical matter, it makes sense to let the airline staff know if you have a disability, especially if you need assistance, for example, in boarding or with seating, because they can have people waiting at the curb or the check-in counter to assist you.

2. Air carriers may not require a person with a disability to travel with an attendant unless the airline deems it necessary for safety reasons. In the case of MS, this might include a person with such severe mobility impairments that she could not assist in her evacuation from the plane. If the airline does require an attendant, the disabled passenger may not be charged for the cost of the attendant's ticket.

3. Service animals must be allowed to travel in the cabin beside the disabled traveler, even if this means that other passengers' seating has to be changed. To avoid questions about the status of an animal, bring proof of its service use or have it outfitted in an appropriate harness.

4. People with disabilities must be allowed to sit in any seat that can accommodate them; they may not be segregated in the airplane. There are some exceptions for people with certain kinds of conditions who must sit in areas such as the bulkheads, which have more leg room. Also, safety regulations restrict seating in exit rows for people who could not help in an emergency evacuation.

5. Airline personnel sometimes are confused about what to do about mobility aids with batteries. Wheelchairs and scooters with spillable batteries are subject to special safety requirements for shipping. But most chair and scooter batteries are now gel cell or nonspillable and may be shipped as baggage or (in theory) brought on board and used. Most chairs or scooters are too wide to bring into the cabin. However, if they can be stowed folded or disassembled in closets with the batteries attached, they will be given priority over other passengers' carry-ons if the disabled traveler takes advantage of the preboarding opportunity. When a device cannot be accommodated in the cabin, the airline must transport it, giving it priority over other cargo and delivering it either to baggage claim or to the aircraft door, as the passenger requests.

6. In no event may mobility devices—chairs, canes, and so forth—be counted as part of a passenger's two-bag carry-on limit. Nor may airlines charge for their packing and shipping. Mobility devices must be returned to the passenger in the condition in which they were delivered to the carrier. Should they be returned in an inoperable state, the airline is obligated to secure alternate transportation and/or accommodations until the device is fixed.

7. Some of the major airlines have specified departments or trained personnel to help people with disabilities, and you may be referred to them if you indicate that you have a disability when you make a reservation. In some cases, they will assign an attendant to meet you at the curb or at the check-in desk and to assist you through the baggage check-in process and through security. You can expect to go through the same security screening as anyone else, but a helpful attendant can sometimes speed the process and help answer questions about such things as mobility devices and prescription drugs. Be sure to comply with the current regulations concerning carry-on items, including (at this writing) the segregation of liquids into small transparent bags. You can get up-to-date information at www.tsa.gov.

As with most things in life, some carriers are better than others. Do not assume that your needs are automatically going to be met if you have not spelled them out in advance, preferably double-checking by phone before leaving for a flight. Disabled travelers still report considerable variation in the quality of service. Even within a company, a "trained" staff in one airport may not be as sharp and efficient as its counterparts at the other end of a journey. As for commuter lines or connections, unless you are familiar with the route and the airport, anyone with mobility problems should find out what she will face before arriving at the departure gate.

Air travel for people with disabilities has been simplified through this law, but do not minimize the importance of prior planning, particularly if you need special help.

A Sea Cruise?

If you decide to skip the hassles of air travel and take a leisurely ocean cruise, you may still be entitled to some legal protection. In a 2005 case, the U.S. Supreme Court ruled that the Americans with Disabilities Act (ADA) does apply to foreign flag cruise ships in U.S. waters. Cruise ships are public accommodations and transportation under the ADA, and are therefore subject to "reasonable modifications" to make them accessible to the disabled to the extent these modifications are "readily achievable." The Court recognized that ADA application here was subject to international laws and treaties. Nevertheless, it seems safe to assume that cruise lines and other such businesses will take actions to comply with the ADA.

Getting Around on the Ground

Getting around in our cities may be just as challenging as flying for someone with a disability. Title II of the ADA covers public transportation. This includes city bus, city rail, ferry, subway, Amtrak, and commuter rail systems.

The application of this law is fairly technical, with a phase-in over many years to allow for modifications of existing stations, buses, and rail cars. The key point here is that public transportation authorities may not discriminate against persons with disabilities in providing services.

Newly purchased public vehicles and newly constructed stations must be accessible to people who use a wheelchair. Used or remanufactured buses must be accessible. Unless it would be an undue burden, paratransit—transportation services for people who are unable to use regular carrier systems—must be made available where there is a fixed-route rail or bus line. Paratransit may include small van and taxi services. In rail services, at least one car per train must be accessible to people who use a wheelchair.

In geographic areas that have public transportation, interested people should contact the local transit authority for particular information on services. Unfortunately, in many locations, accessible transportation, even paratransit services, remains unavailable or of substandard quality. Consumer vigilance is always required. For more information and to file transportation complaints contact:

Office of Civil Rights
Federal Transit Administration
US Department of Transportation
400 Seventh Street, SW
Washington, DC 20590

ADA information, questions, and complaints:
888-446-4511 (voice/relay);
Internet address: www.fta.dot.gov/ada
Note: private transportation services such as private bus lines, taxicabs, and vans are covered by Title III of the ADA (see following section).

USING PUBLIC ACCOMMODATIONS

The 1990 ADA requires that people with medical problems such as MS have access to public accommodations, including buildings or other facilities operated by state and local government agencies or by private owners who open them to the public. Regulations provide a list of examples of physical or mental impairments that qualify as "disabilities." This list includes MS.

Access requirements—barrier removal, architectural modifications, relocation of programs, or expansion of communication and transportation services—are intended to ensure the full participation of the disabled subject to considerations of undue financial and administrative burdens. Older buildings must be modified or programs moved to make them accessible to the public; new buildings must comply with federal standards for accessibility. ADA architectural standards also apply to public accommodations and commercial facilities covered by Title III. There is an exception for historic sites if accommodation would threaten their character. But, here again, other methods of ensuring access by people with disabilities would have to be devised. The U.S. Supreme Court has ruled that it was a violation of the ADA for a courthouse to limit access to people in a wheelchair. And it was not sufficient if the county offered to have someone carry the disabled person into the courtroom. As a result of this and similar rulings, some public buildings have had to be rebuilt or substantially modified.

Title III of the ADA prohibits discrimination on the basis of disability in public accommodations and commercial facilities. This covers entities that own, lease, lease to, or operate facilities that include businesses, restaurants, medical offices, theaters, private schools, museums, sports arenas, daycare centers, and retail stores, to name but a few.

Commercial facilities that are covered include factories, office buildings, warehouses, and any entity that affects commerce. Private entities that offer training, certification, licensing, applications, and examinations must provide them in accessible settings.

Hotel, motels, and inns generally are covered under the ADA, with an exception for small lodgings such as bed-and-breakfasts. *Note:* private residences do not come within the scope of Title III of the ADA unless they also are being used as businesses; for example, an accounting office located in one part of a home. In that type of situation, those areas of the house that are used in the business, such as entrances and walkways, must meet Title III requirements.

Title III and its regulations contain detailed building requirements for both new and existing structures. These requirements cover a wide range of site elements, including bathrooms, entrances, phone installations, teller machines, check-out stands, fixed seating, ramps, signage, drinking fountains, and control mechanisms. Additional guidelines, called "scoping requirements," detail when and how many of certain elements need to be located in new construction. For example, every public or common use bathroom must have at least one stall that is accessible; two, if there are six or more stalls. Another example: at least 50 percent of all entrances must be accessible, including parking garages, tunnels, and overhead walkways.

The basic goal of these provisions is that architectural barriers must be removed in existing facilities unless doing so would be an undue burden. New or altered facilities must comply with the ADA Accessibility Guidelines. When alterations are made, those that affect a "primary function area"—a doorway, a lobby, a bathroom, telephones, walkways, and so forth—must be made accessible unless the added costs of compliance are disproportionate to the total cost of the alterations. By law, costs in excess of 20 percent of the original plan are considered disproportionate (see the Appendix).

Equipment and other facilities also must be accessible. One of the more important requirements concerns elevators. Generally, elevators *are* required in a new building occupied after January 26, 1993. However, they are *not* required in facilities under three stories or with fewer than 3,000 square feet per floor unless the building is used as a shopping center, shopping mall, professional office of a health care provider, or public transportation station.

Title III and its regulations are full of examples of possible accessibility problems and acceptable, readily achievable solutions. These include making curb cuts, installing ramps, widening doorways, or rearranging furniture so that a wheelchair can pass through. As with much of the rest of the law, Congress envisioned a case-by-case approach to determining how this and other portions of the ADA should be enforced. Anything that has the effect of segregating, excluding, or reducing access and service is permissible *only* in very narrowly construed circumstances. For example, a small retail store might not be required to rearrange furniture or merchandise to make it accessible if it would have the effect of significantly reducing sales.

There is no obligation imposed on a business to provide devices such as eyeglasses, wheelchairs, or hearing aids or to provide personal attendant services in order to be in compliance. Policies may need to be changed or relaxed, however, to allow for equal opportunity. Stores that allow only one person at a time in a dressing room may have to allow an attendant to accompany a disabled individual if it is necessary for that person to be able to shop for clothes. Another example: service animals may have to be allowed in a commercial facility even though nondisabled people would not be able to bring in their pets. In a 1997 Texas case, a blind man successfully challenged a brewery that refused to let him take his guide dog on a tour even though the company argued that this was in violation of health and safety codes.

Safety requirements may restrict people with disabilities in some settings. A typical example in the regulations might be a height requirement on certain rides at an amusement park. What about restricting a person in a scooter from the same ride? There is no set rule. Each case must be considered on its own merits, with potential remedies tied to the resources of the business; meaning a mom-and-pop store should have a lighter compliance burden than a Fortune 500 company.

Help in Communicating

Getting around today often means having access to electronic methods of communication as much as it does physical movement. Title IV of the ADA deals with telephone and television access for people with hearing and speech impairments. Phone companies must establish 24-hour-a-day, 7-day-a-week interstate and intrastate telecommunications relay services so that individuals with speech or hearing impairments can communicate with people who use regular voice phones. Title IV also requires closed captioning of federally funded public service announcements. The Federal Communications Commission regulates Title IV standards. The address is:

FCC
445 12th Street, SW
Washington, DC 20554
(888) 225-5322 (voice); (888) 835-5322 (TTY)
www.fcc.gov/cgb.dro

In addition to the ADA's enforcement of relay services, two laws from the late 1990s address access by the disabled to telecommunications products and services. The first is Section 508, an amendment to the Rehabilitation Act of 1973. Section 508 requires the federal government to ensure that technology is accessible to employees and the public except where that would create an "undue burden." Complaints are to be filed with the agency alleged to be noncompliant.

The Telecommunications Act of 1996 requires technology and equipment manufacturers and service providers to make products and services accessible to people with disabilities. Where access is not readily achievable, Section 255 of this act requires manufacturers and service providers to make devices and services compatible with services and equipment commonly used by people with disabilities. This act is enforced by the FCC (see www.fcc.gov/cgb/complaints). Telephone: 1-888 CALL-FCC (1-888-225-5322); 1-888 TELL-FCC (835-5322 TTY); fax 1-866 418 0232; e-mail fcc.info@fcc.gov.

Taking Part

Your right to access is not limited to building design or the layout of facilities. At least in the case of governmental or tax-supported agencies, programs and activities intended for general participation must show consideration for those with disabilities.

Services, programs, and activities must be provided in an integrated setting unless separate measures are necessary in order to deliver equal opportunity. For example, although a special tour of an art museum may be offered to someone who is blind, the blind person could not be forced to use the special tour—it would be a choice, not a requirement. Eligibility standards or rules that have the effect of screening out people with disabilities from activities must also be eliminated unless it can be shown that they are necessary. An example might be requiring driver's licenses as opposed to another kind of picture I.D. for identification when some disabled people are unable to drive. Safety requirements *may* be imposed if they are necessary to ensure the safe provision of services, but these must be based on objective standards, not on stereotypes or fears about disability. Setting down certain eligibility requirements for driver's licenses themselves is permitted even though that will preclude some disabled people from operating vehicles.

A "qualified individual with a disability" is someone who meets the essential eligibility requirements for a particular program or activity. The definition of "essential eligibility requirements" varies depending on the program or activity involved. In those instances in which the governmental entity provides information or services to the public at large, "essential eligibility requirements" should be minimal. Title II of the ADA requires reasonable modifications in state or local government policies, practices, and procedures when necessary to provide equal opportunity unless it can be shown that to do so would fundamentally alter the nature of the service, program, or activity in question. The public entity would still have to develop alternate means to ensure that disabled people receive the benefits or services.

Public entities must furnish auxiliary aids and services—interpreters, readers, telephone devices for the deaf, and so forth—to ensure effective communication with the disabled. Emergency services such as 911 must provide appropriate access for individuals with speech and hearing disabilities, but there is no requirement that wheelchairs, glasses, attendants, or other similar devices or assistance for personal use be provided.

A state or local government may choose to provide additional services or special benefits to people with disabilities, but no one may be required to use them. For example, a person with a cane may not be required to enter a building by way of the wheelchair ramp. People who have disabilities may not be charged for the costs of inclusion, whether that means the price of structural modifications or the salary of interpreters. In general, churches and other religious organizations are not covered under the ADA, although they may be subject to similar state statutes. Neither are private clubs unless they are made available to the public. In the highly publicized case involving disabled golfer Casey Martin and the PGA, Martin won the right to use a golf cart in professional tournaments by claiming that tournaments played at private golf clubs were, in fact, a public accommodation under Title III.

Much of the language of Title III duplicates that of Title II. The definition of "individuals with disabilities" is the same, with MS again listed in the regulations as an example of a physical or mental impairment that limits "major life activities." Public accommodations must provide services in an integrated setting unless separate services are needed to ensure equal opportunity, which rarely should be the case. As with Title II, they must make reasonable modifications to policies, practices, and procedures to allow for the participation of people with disabilities unless to do so would fundamentally alter the nature of the goods and services. The first priority of Title III in accessibility is ensuring that people who are disabled can "get in the front door," followed by such modifications, alterations, and changes as are needed to enable full use of facilities and services. Eligibility standards that prevent disabled individuals from equally receiving goods and services must be eliminated unless they are necessary for safety reasons. Auxiliary aids to facilitate effective communication must be provided unless to do so would cause an undue burden or a fundamental alteration of the service.

COMING HOME

A popular song tells us "there's a place for us, somewhere a place. . . ." Unfortunately, this is not always the case for people with a real or perceived disability. Once again, the law seeks to redress the balance.

The Fair Housing Amendments Act of 1988 (the FHAA) (see 42 USC 3601 *et seq.*) prohibits discrimination in housing based on family status—children in the household, adults who are not related by blood or marriage—and handicap (the FHAA uses the word *handicap* instead of *disability*). This was an expansion of the protections of the Fair Housing Act of 1968, which banned discrimination in housing on the basis of race or color, national origin, religion, and sex; and on Section 504 of the Rehabilitation Act of 1973, which prohibited discrimination on the basis of disability in housing that received federal financial assistance.

The definition of *handicap* is essentially the same as that of *disability* in the Americans with Disabilities Act. A person with a handicap is any person who

1) has a physical or mental impairment which substantially limits one or more of such person's major life activities,
2) a record of such an impairment, or
3) being regarded as having such an impairment.

MS is listed in the FHAA's regulations as an example of a physical impairment.

Under the FHAA, no one may refuse to sell, rent, or make available a house, apartment, or other dwelling on the basis of a buyer's or renter's handicap. It also is illegal to discriminate on the basis of the handicap of someone associated with a buyer or renter; for example, a spouse who uses a wheelchair. The FHAA prohibits discrimination because of the handicap of anyone living or planning to live in the dwelling. This last prohibition is aimed in part at zoning or deed restrictions that seek to limit small group homes in single-family residential areas for people with disabilities. Different terms, conditions, and privileges on the sale or rental of a dwelling may not be imposed on the basis of handicap, such as increased interest rates or fees for a loan.

Much of the housing in this country is covered by the Act. But single-family houses sold or rented without the use of a broker or agent are exempted, as are owner-occupied dwellings with four or fewer units. Discrimination through advertisements or other notices of sale or rental of any property, whether oral or in writing, is prohibited.

The FHAA places limitations on presale or rental inquiries. In general, a seller or landlord may not ask about a handicap or its severity. But he may ask if a prospective buyer or renter can meet the requirements of the transaction—for example, does the tenant have the ability to make the monthly payments? He also may ask if a would-be tenant is a current illegal drug user. In some instances in which priority may be given to a person with a handicap, or where a handicap is required—as in certain government-funded housing for the disabled—the existence of a handicap obviously must be established.

Nothing in the FHAA requires the seller of a single-family home to make the house accessible. However, one of the key provisions of the law concerns modifications to rental property. A landlord may not refuse to let a person with a handicap make reasonable modifications to a dwelling or its common areas if necessary for her use. Usually these modifications are at the disabled person's expense, and the property must be restored to its original condition at the end of the lease, with normal wear and tear excepted. Not all modifications must be restored. For example, grab bars installed in a bathroom may need to be removed when a tenant moves out, but structural reinforcement of the wall to support the bars would not interfere with the next tenant's use, so this modification does not have to be taken out. Along the same lines, a widened doorway to permit the passage of a wheelchair would not interfere with the landlord's or a later tenant's use and therefore would not have to be restored to the original condition.

A landlord may require a tenant to provide a description of any work to be done, with reasonable assurances that it will be carried out in an acceptable manner with all building permits obtained, if required. A landlord may not increase the rent or the security deposit as a condition for modifications, but he may negotiate a restoration agreement with a provision that requires the tenant to pay, over a reasonable time, into an interest-bearing escrow account, an amount of money sufficient to cover expected restoration costs. Any interest from the account belongs to the tenant.

Not all modifications under the FHAA require much if any cost. Landlords must make reasonable changes in rules, policies, practices, or services so that the premises are fully usable to a disabled tenant. Examples could include changing a "no pets" policy to allow the use of service animals or providing a reserved parking spot for a mobility-impaired person who might otherwise be unable to use a common parking lot.

The FHAA contains construction requirements for new multifamily dwellings with four or more units, ready for first occupancy after March 13, 1991. Each building must have at least one accessible entrance unless that is impractical because of the unusual characteristics of the terrain or site. Public and common areas must be accessible. Hallways and doors must be wide enough for wheelchairs, and there must be an accessible pathway to and through a unit. Bathroom walls must be reinforced to allow the installation of grab bars. Electrical outlets must be placed so that they are accessible to someone using a wheelchair. Kitchens and bathrooms must be large enough to permit a person in a wheelchair to maneuver in them.

Nothing in the FHAA limits state and local governments from requiring more extensive accessibility standards. In a few places, local ordinances require all new residential construction, including single-family houses that are built using public funds, to conform to accessibility standards comparable to those in the FHAA. Contact local housing authorities for information about your area.

Financial Help In Housing

For some people, MS progresses to the point where they need help to cope with the requirements of daily living. In the past, the principal public source of funding for this kind of help was Medicaid payments to a nursing home facility for those who qualified based on disability and on limited financial resources (see Chapter 6).

Many people would prefer an alternative that would allow them to receive help in their own home. It is now becoming more recognized that this is important to the disabled person, and that it may save money for the government programs which may be responsible for payment. Therefore, there is now a trend against segregating the disabled population, but instead allowing community-based programs for dealing with their needs. This trend was reinforced by a suit in Georgia called the Olmstead case, which held that public entities like the state departments of health cannot discriminate against the disabled by unjustified segregation. In other words, the ADA requires that public agencies provide services "in the most integrated setting appropriate to the needs of the qualified individuals with disabilities."

As a result of this case, and the Deficit Reduction Act of 2005, the federal Centers for Medicare and Medicaid Services (CMS) began to work with states through grants, funding changes, and pilot projects to develop initiatives to help people who are inappropriately placed in institutions under Medicaid. These efforts are often called "Money follows the person" (MFP) initiatives, the idea being that their Medicaid funds can follow them and be used to pay for community services. These initiatives are better developed in some states than others, with shorter waiting lists and more community-based alternatives. This is a movement that is at the forefront of disability activities nationwide. It is not difficult to imagine what some of the barriers to community living for a person on Medicaid can be. For example, affordable accessible housing is often hard to find. Nevertheless, some states have made real progress in moving people out of Medicaid-funded institutions and back into the community. The specific mechanisms for accomplishing the MFP goals vary from state-to-state based on a number of factors such as legislative budgeting and identifying appropriate candidates for transfer back to the home or community. This is a movement which is likely to continue to advance as a way to integrate people back into society. To research MFP activities in your state, contact your state health department, the National Multiple Sclerosis Society (NMSS), and/or your local NMSS office.

ENFORCING YOUR RIGHTS TO ACCESS ADA

Title III (public accommodations and commercial facilities) may be enforced by private lawsuits to obtain a court order to stop discrimination. It is not necessary to file a complaint before bringing suit; there is no "right-to-sue" letter requirement. Although attorney's fees may be awarded, an individual bringing the suit may not receive monetary damages. An individual also may file a complaint, and the Attorney General is authorized to sue in cases of public interest or to stop a pattern or practice of discrimination. In a Department of Justice (DOJ) suit, the court may impose civil penalties of up to $50,000 for a first violation; $100,000 for any later violation, as well as damages. The penalties go to the government, not to the person complaining.

The DOJ handles complaints under Title II (state and local governments), which must be filed within 180 days of the date of the alleged violation. Complaints may also be filed with federal agencies that fund, regulate, or administer part of the state or local programs, services, or activities in question. These include the Departments of Agriculture, Education, Health and Human Services, Housing and Urban Development, Interior, and Labor. Both individuals and classes of individuals may file a complaint.

After an investigation and an attempt to resolve a complaint, including possible referral to mediation, the DOJ may file suit to enforce the law. Individuals do not have to file a complaint first with the DOJ or other federal agency or obtain a "right-to-sue" letter before bringing their own private lawsuit under Title II. If successful under Title II, they may receive money damages and attorney's fees.

It is discrimination for anyone to retaliate, interfere with, coerce, or intimidate a person who brings a charge under the ADA. It also is unlawful to discriminate against any person, disabled or not, who assists someone in pursuing his rights under the ADA. Remedies for retaliation, coercion, and so forth are those provided by the particular title involved. The winning party in any ADA action also may be awarded expenses and costs at the court's discretion.

For information on filing a complaint under Title II or III contact

Disability Rights Section
Civil Rights Division
US Department of Justice
950 Pennsylvania Avenue, NW NYNV
Washington, DC 20530
(800) 514-0301 (voice); (800) 514-0383 (TDD)
www.us.doj.gov/crt/ada/adahom1.htm

AIR TRAVEL

Claims for damage, loss, or other complaints under the Air Carrier Access Act may be directed to the compliance resolution official of each carrier at the airport or to:

US Department of Transportation
Office of Consumer Affairs
400 7th Street, SW
Washington, DC 20590

Office for Civil Rights:
(202) 366-4648 (voice); (202) 366-8538 (TDD)

Aviation Consumer Protection Division:
(202) 366-2220 (voice); (202) 755-7687 (TDD)
airconsumer.ost.dot.gov

HOUSING

The Department of Housing and Urban Development (HUD) administers the FHAA. Complaints may be filed with the Office of Fair Housing and Equal Opportunity of HUD, Washington, D.C. (see address and telephone number) or through a regional fair housing office. In some instances, HUD may refer the complaint to a state or local agency with comparable authority. Other federal government agencies may also have jurisdiction to handle some housing discrimination complaints if they involve programs administered by that agency.

Complaints must be filed within 1 year of the alleged violation. HUD will investigate the complaint and attempt to reach a conciliation agreement among the parties that will also protect the interests of similarly situated persons and the public's interest in seeing the goals of the FHAA carried out. If there is no resolution, the complaint may go before an administrative law judge (ALJ) for hearing. When irreparable harm could result if an FHAA violation is not immediately handled, HUD may request the Attorney General to seek protective orders pending the outcome of the investigation. Likewise, should a conciliation agreement be breached, HUD will refer the matter to the Attorney General.

Remedies may include actual damages, including damages for humiliation, pain and suffering, injunctive relief, and attorney's fees. Civil penalties payable to the federal government may also be assessed.

For more information or to file a complaint:

Disability Rights Section
Civil Rights Division

US Department of Justice
950 Pennsylvania Avenue, NW
Washington DC 20590
(202) 708-1112 (voice); (202) 708-1455 (TTY)
(800) 669-9777 (voice); (800) 927-9275 (TTY)

A complaining party also has the right to file her own suit in lieu of going through the administrative hearing process; such suits must be filed within 2 years of the alleged act of discrimination. As with the ADA and FMLA, the FHAA protects people from threats or retaliation for filing a complaint or assisting someone in asserting his rights. For complaint information, contact:

US Department of Housing and Urban Development
Office of Program Compliance and Disability Rights
Office of Fair Housing and Equal Opportunity
451 7th Street, SW (Room 5204)
Washington, DC 20140
(800) 669-9777 (voice); (800) 927-9275 (TYY)
www.hud.gov/offices/fheo

For questions about accessibility under the Fair Housing Act:
(888) 341-7781 (voice/relay)
www.fairhousingfirst.org
Publications: (800) 767-7468 (voice/relay)

12
Helpful Web Sites

I N ADDITION TO WEB SITES AND TELEPHONE NUMBERS previously listed, the following represent sources for helpful information as well as links to other sites. This is by no means a complete list of disability-related sites, and it is important to remember that web sites and telephone numbers change all the time. But it's a good way to start branching out on your own.

- **www.aoa.gov/ownyourfuture** US Department of Health and Human Services site for planning and paying for long-term care services. (866) 752-6582. This is not at all depressing, but is a way realistically to think about possible future needs and how to deal with them.
- **www.ssa.gov/best/** The Benefit Eligibility Screening Tool (BEST) is a quick way to go online and start to figure out what government benefits like Medicare and Medicaid you might be eligible for.
- Check out many other government web sites including **Medicare.gov, MyMedicare.gov, SocialSecurity.gov.** Also, different departmental web sites can give you links to many other sites of interest.
- **www.dhhs.gov** (Department of Health and Human Services)
- **www.usdoj.gov** (Department of Justice)
- **www.ada.gov** (Americans with Disabilities Act)

- **www.section508.gov** (amendment to the Rehabilitation Act of 1973 setting out requirements for making electronic and information technology accessible
- **www.USSupremeCourt.gov**
- **www.dol.gov** (Department of Labor)
- **www.dot.gov** (Department of Transportation)
- **www.tsa.gov** (Transportation Safety Administration—travel information for the disabled, especially air travel security updates)
- **www.usa.gov** A general government web site organized by subject into other web sites—a good way to expand research
- **www.va.gov** (Department of Veterans Affairs-anyone who is a vereran or has a veteran in his family should check on benefits, including long term care benefits.
- **www.eeoc.gov** This agency interprets and enforces ADA requirements related to employment
- **www.nationalmssociety.org** A good source, obviously, for all kinds of important news relating to multiple sclerosis and its management. There are a lot of links to resources you may have never considered.
- **Abledata.com** Lots of information about wheelchairs, scooters, and similar equipment to research on your own without third-party (sales, therapist, or other) interference.
- **www.wildernessinquiry.org** Possibly the most beautiful web site we've ever seen for outdoor adventure vacations all over the world, aimed at everyone, including the disabled. The group states that they are committed to helping all people enjoy the wilderness and they have some financial assistance available.

Other great resources are the Independent Living Centers. It may be worthwhile to get on the mailing or e-mail list of the nearest center. In some states, the centers will have different names which makes it difficult to find them from the phone book. Go to www.ilru.org for a directory. The centers serve a range of disabilities and needs and have some of the most knowledgeable staffers, especially on local and state resources, to assist you.

Glossary

ABC Drugs: A common term for the multiple sclerosis drugs Avonex (interferon beta- 1a; Biogen Idec, Cambridge, MA), Betaseron (interferon beta-1b; Berlex Laboratories, Montville, NJ), and Copaxone (glatiramer; Teva, Pharmaceuticals, Petah Tikva, Israel).

Chapter 7: A type of bankruptcy, sometimes called a "straight" bankruptcy, that discharges or wipes out most debts.

Chapter 13: A type of bankruptcy, sometimes called a "wage-earner plan," that allows most debts to be paid off over time.

Community property: The system for determining ownership of property in a marriage in several states; in general, property acquired with earned income during a marriage belongs equally to both spouses.

Common law: The system of law for determining ownership of property in a marriage in most states.

Disability: Physical or mental limitations; in the Social Security context, a complete inability to engage in full-time, substantial gainful activity. For purposes of the Americans with Disabilities Act, an impairment that affects one or more of the major life activities, a history of such an impairment, or being regarded by others as having such an impairment.

Disability insurance: Insurance, either purchased by an individual or provided by an employer, that pays income in the event of disability.

Fee-for-service: Sometimes called "indemnity" coverage. this was until recently the most common form of private health care, with beneficiaries able to choose their own doctors and hospitals, and generally requiring a co-payment of the cost of health-care services.

Managed care: The most common form of health-care coverage (e.g., health maintenance organizations [HMOs], preferred provider organizations [PPOs]), which limits to some extent the ability of the beneficiary to choose doctors, hospitals, and treatments, but perhaps at a lower cost than fee-for-service coverage.

Medicaid: Government-provided medical coverage for people who are impoverished and eligible for Supplemental Security Income.

Medicare: Medical coverage provided by the federal government for the elderly and for people who have been eligible for Social Security Disability Insurance for at least 24 months.

> **Medicare Part A:** Provides hospitalization insurance for people covered by Medicare.

> **Medicare Part B:** Provides payment for doctor visits and other out-of-hospital costs for people covered by Medicare.

> **Medicare Part C:** Provides Medicare recipients with the option (but not the obligation) to be covered by HMO- or PPO-type organizations.

> **Medicare Part D:** A recent (2006) Medicare benefit which provides coverage for outpatient drugs as part of a program offered by various private insurance companies.

"Money follows the person": A term which describes a concept where in some government-sponsored benefits, such as access to nursing care, may be available through a variety of formats, such as private nursing homes, in-home care, and other programs. Currently, these programs are still in the trial stage in many states.

Personal property: Generally, an individual's possessions other than real estate such as cash, clothes, stocks, furniture, car, and so forth.

Power of attorney: A document that grants another person the power to act in the place of the person who gives the power in business, financial, legal, or health matters.

> **General power of attorney:** A power that allows someone to act on behalf of the person who gives the authority in any matter

Special power of attorney: A power that is given for a specific limited purpose, such as for the sale of a house.

Health care power of attorney/advance directive for health care/medical directive/health care proxy: Particular names of these powers vary from state-to-state; they grant another person the power to make health-care decisions when the person who gives the authority is unable to do so for himself.

Living will: Sometimes called a "directive to physicians," this document expresses a person's wishes regarding medical care in the event that he is terminally ill and unable to communicate.

Irrevocable power of attorney: A power of attorney that cannot be undone.

Real estate: Real property such as a house or land; this kind of property may be subject to treatment different from that of personal property, depending on the type of legal action involved; for example, divorce or bankruptcy.

Scheduled and unscheduled debt: For the purposes of Chapter 7 or 13, debts that are listed or not listed in the paperwork filed in a bankruptcy proceeding.

Secured debt: Debt for which collateral has been pledged, usually a specific piece of property such as a house, car, or boat; the property may be repossessed in the event of nonpayment of the debt

Social Security Disability Insurance (SSDI): Income available to individuals who meet the total disability standard of the Social Security Administration and who have paid the required number of credits through payroll taxes (FICA).

Supplemental Security Income (SSI): Income available to totally disabled individuals based on financial need.

Tax deduction/tax credit: A deduction is a reduction in a person's taxable income; a credit is a direct reduction in the amount of taxes owed.

Tort: A wrongful act, damage, or injury for which one may sue; differs from a contract, which is an agreement between two or more parties (persons).

Trust: Property given to a person, usually for the use or benefit of another.

Resources

Americans with Disability Act (ADA)

For questions regarding accessibility issues under the Architectural Barriers Act (federal facilities and post offices) or the ADA Accessibility Guidelines, contact the Access Board or Architectural and Transportation Barriers Compliance Board at:

- Documents and questions: (800) 872-2253 (voice); (800) 993-2822 (TDD)
- Internet address: www.access-board.gov/

For technical ADA assistance including publications, contact one of the Department of Education's 10 regional Disability & Business Technical Assistance Centers.

- The (800) number will connect you to the center in your area: (800) 949-4232 (voice/TDD)
- Internet address: www.adata.org

For employment questions, contact the President's Committee on Employment of People with Disabilities.

- (202) 376-6200 (voice); (202) 376-6205 (TDD)
- Internet address: www.pcepd.gov

For advice on accommodating employees with disabilities, contact the Job Accommodation Network (JAN).

- (800) 526-7234 (voice/TDD)
- Internet address: janweb.icdi.wvu.edu/english/homeus.htm
- For information on tax code provisions relating to disability like tax credits (Sec 44) and deductions (Sec. 190), contact the Internal Revenue Service (IRS)
- Tax code information: (800) 829-1040 (voice); (800) 829-4059 (TDD)
- Tax code legal questions: (202) 622-3110 (voice); TDD: use relay service
- To order Publications 535 and 334: (800) 829-2676 (voice); (800) 829-4059 (TDD)
- Department of Justice ADA Hotline: (800) 466-4232 (voice/TDD)
- Project Action, funded by the Department of Transportation, provides information and publications on ADA accessibility; (800) 659-6429 (voice); TDD: use relay service (202) 347-3066 (voice); (202) 347-7385 (TDD)

HEALTH, DISABILITY, AND ADVOCACY ORGANIZATIONS

National Multiple Sclerosis Society
733 Third Avenue
New York, NY 10017-3288
(212) 986-3240
(800) FIGHT MS (1-800-344-4867) Information
Internet address: www.nmss.org; E-mail address: editor@nmss.org

National Council on Independent Living (NCIL)
1916 Wilson Boulevard, Suite 209
Arlington, VA 22201
(703) 525-3406 (voice); (703) 525-4153 (TTY)
E-mail: ncil@tsbbs02.tnet.com

Independent Living Centers exist throughout the country to provide training, advocacy, information, and assistance to people with disabilities.

National Organization of Social Security Claimants' Representatives
6 Prospect Street
Midland Park, NJ 07432
(201) 444-1415; FAX (201) 444-1823
(800) 431-2804
Internet address: www.NOSSCR.org; NOSSCR@Worldnet.att.net

Lawyer trade group provides information and referral on Social Security claims.

Paralyzed Veterans of America
801 18th Street, NW
Washington, DC 20006
(800) 424-8200
Internet address: www.pva.org

This organization has been especially active in accessibility issues nationwide; the web site contains information on many topics of interest to the disabled.

Financial Planning Assistance

Internet address: thearc.org.welcome.html
ARC (formerly Association for Retarded Citizens) may be a resource for information on Medicaid (nursing home) qualifications for people with disabilities, not just the retarded. In a few states, ARC and/or other nonprofit organizations administer pooled supplemental needs trusts which allow people to maintain their Medicaid eligibility while still receiving income above what would otherwise be permitted. See The ARC of Texas for more information:

1600 West 38th Street, Suite 200
Austin, TX 78731
(800) 252-9729
Internet address: www.thearcoftexas.org

National Academy for Elder Law Attorneys, Inc.
1604 North Country Club Road
Tucson, AZ 85716
(520) 881-4005
Internet address: www.naela.org

This organization publishes consumer guides on a wide range of topics of interest to the elderly (and the disabled) such as, for example, like Medicaid, Medicare, guardianships, living wills, powers of attorney, and trusts. It also can provide (at a cost) lists of member attorneys throughout the country. *The NAELA does not make referrals.*

Housing

National Accessible Apartment Clearinghouse
201 North Union Street, Suite 200
Alexandria, VA 22314
(800) 421-1221
Fax: (703) 518-6191
Internet address: www.aptsforrent.com/naac; clearninghouse@naahq.com

National database of accessible apartments in 155 metropolitan areas; provides free assistance to the disabled in locating housing that fits their specific needs.

Additional Internet Resources

- Medicaid and Medicare information: www.hcfa.gov/
- Federal statutes and proposed legislation: thomas.loc.gov/
- Federal rules: www.gpoaccess.gov/cfr/index.html
- Health related information: www.healthfinder.gov
- State-by-state health insurance information: data.georgetown.edu/research/ihcrp/hipaa
- gucfm.cfm.georgetown.edu/ihcrp.html (Georgetown University Institute for Health Care Research and Policy)
- Martindale-Hubbell Legal Directory: www.martindale.com/locator
- US House of Representatives library: law.house.gov/
- Disability-related laws: law.house.gov/102.htm

Appendix

U.S. Department of Labor

Employment Standards Administration Wage and Hour Division

Fact Sheet #28: The Family and Medical Leave Act of 1993

THE FAMILY AND MEDICAL LEAVE ACT OF 1993

The U.S. Department of Labor's Employment Standards Administration, Wage and Hour Division, administers and enforces the Family and Medical Leave Act (FMLA) for all private, state and local government employees, and some federal employees. Most Federal and certain congressional employees are also covered by the law and are subject to the jurisdiction of the U.S. Office of Personnel Management or the Congress.

FMLA became effective on August 5, 1993, for most employers. If a collective bargaining agreement (CBA) was in effect on that date, FMLA became effective on the expiration date of the CBA or February 5, 1994, whichever was earlier. FMLA entitles eligible employees to take up to 12 weeks of unpaid, job-protected leave in a 12-month period for specified family and medical reasons. The employer may elect to use the calendar year, a fixed 12-month leave or fiscal year, or a 12-month period prior to or after the commencement of leave as the 12-month period.

The law contains provisions on employer coverage; employee eligibility for the law's benefits; entitlement to leave, maintenance of health benefits during leave, and job restoration after leave; notice and certification of the need for FMLA leave; and, protection for employees who request or take FMLA leave. The law also requires employers to keep certain records.

EMPLOYER COVERAGE

FMLA applies to all:

- public agencies, including state, local and federal employers, local education agencies (schools), **and**
- private-sector employers who employed 50 or more employees in 20 or more workweeks in the current or preceding calendar year **and** who are engaged in commerce or in any industry or activity affecting commerce — including joint employers and successors of covered employers.

EMPLOYEE ELIGIBILITY

To be eligible for FMLA benefits, an employee **must**:

1. work for a covered employer;
2. have worked for the employer for a total of 12 months*;
3. have worked at least 1,250 hours over the previous 12 months*; and
4. work at a location in the United States or in any territory or possession of the United States where at least 50 employees are employed by the employer within 75 miles.

* See special rules for returning reservists under USERRA.

LEAVE ENTITLEMENT

A covered employer must grant an eligible employee up to a total of 12 workweeks of **unpaid** leave during any 12-month period for one or more of the following reasons:

- for the birth and care of the newborn child of the employee;

- for placement with the employee of a son or daughter for adoption or foster care;
- to care for an immediate family member (spouse, child, or parent) with a serious health condition; **or**
- to take medical leave when the employee is unable to work because of a serious health condition.

Spouses employed by the same employer are jointly entitled to a **combined** total of 12 work-weeks of family leave for the birth and care of the newborn child, for placement of a child for adoption or foster care, and to care for a parent who has a serious health condition.

Leave for birth and care, or placement for adoption or foster care must conclude within 12 months of the birth or placement.

Under some circumstances, employees may take FMLA leave intermittently — which means taking leave in blocks of time, or by reducing their normal weekly or daily work schedule.

- If FMLA leave is for birth and care or placement for adoption or foster care, use of intermittent leave is subject to the employer's approval.
- FMLA leave may be taken intermittently whenever **medically necessary** to care for a seriously ill family member, or because the employee is seriously ill and unable to work.

Also, subject to certain conditions, employees **or** employers may choose to use accrued **paid** leave (such as sick or vacation leave) to cover some or all of the FMLA leave.

The employer is responsible for designating if an employee's use of paid leave counts as FMLA leave, based on information from the employee.

"**Serious health condition**" means an illness, injury, impairment, or physical or mental condition that involves either:

- any period of incapacity or treatment connected with inpatient care (i.e., an overnight stay) in a hospital, hospice, or residential medical-care facility, and any period of incapacity or subsequent treatment in connection with such inpatient care; **or**
- Continuing treatment by a health care provider which includes any period of incapacity (i.e., inability to work, attend school or perform other regular daily activities) due to:

(1) A health condition (including treatment therefor, or recovery therefrom) lasting more than three consecutive days, and any subsequent treatment or period of incapacity relating to the same condition, that **also** includes:

- treatment two or more times by or under the supervision of a health care provider; **or**
- one treatment by a health care provider with a continuing regimen of treatment; **or**

(2) Pregnancy or prenatal care. A visit to the health care provider is not necessary for each absence; **or**

(3) A chronic serious health condition which continues over an extended period of time, requires periodic visits to a health care provider, and may involve occasional episodes of incapacity (e.g., asthma, diabetes). A visit to a health care provider is not necessary for each absence; **or**

(4) A permanent or long-term condition for which treatment may not be effective (e.g., Alzheimer's, a severe stroke, terminal cancer). Only supervision by a health care provider is required, rather than active treatment; **or**

(5) Any absences to receive multiple treatments for restorative surgery or for a condition which would likely result in a period of incapacity of more than three days if not treated (e.g., chemotherapy or radiation treatments for cancer).

"**Health care provider**" means:

- doctors of medicine or osteopathy authorized to practice medicine or surgery by the state in which the doctors practice; **or**
- podiatrists, dentists, clinical psychologists, optometrists and chiropractors (limited to manual

manipulation of the spine to correct a subluxation as demonstrated by X-ray to exist) authorized to practice, and performing within the scope of their practice, under state law; **or**

- nurse practitioners, nurse-midwives and clinical social workers authorized to practice, and performing within the scope of their practice, as defined under state law; **or**
- Christian Science practitioners listed with the First Church of Christ, Scientist in Boston, Massachusetts; **or**
- Any health care provider recognized by the employer or the employer's group health plan benefits manager.

MAINTENANCE OF HEALTH BENEFITS

A covered employer is required to maintain group health insurance coverage for an employee on FMLA leave whenever such insurance was provided before the leave was taken and on the same terms as if the employee had continued to work. If applicable, arrangements will need to be made for employees to pay their share of health insurance premiums while on leave.

In some instances, the employer may recover premiums it paid to maintain health coverage for an employee who fails to return to work from FMLA leave.

JOB RESTORATION

Upon return from FMLA leave, an employee must be restored to the employee's original job, or to an equivalent job with equivalent pay, benefits, and other terms and conditions of employment.

In addition, an employee's use of FMLA leave cannot result in the loss of any employment benefit that the employee earned or was entitled to **before** using FMLA leave, nor be counted against the employee under a "no fault" attendance policy.

Under specified and limited circumstances where restoration to employment will cause substantial and grievous economic injury to its operations, an employer may refuse to reinstate certain highly-paid **"key"** employees after using FMLA leave during which health coverage was maintained. In order to do so, the employer must:

- notify the employee of his/her status as a "key" employee in response to the employee's notice of intent to take FMLA leave;
- notify the employee as soon as the employer decides it will deny job restoration, and explain the reasons for this decision;
- offer the employee a reasonable opportunity to return to work from FMLA leave after giving this notice; **and**
- make a final determination as to whether reinstatement will be denied at the end of the leave period if the employee then requests restoration.

A **"key"** employee is a salaried "eligible" employee who is among the highest paid ten percent of employees within 75 miles of the work site.

NOTICE AND CERTIFICATION

Employees seeking to use FMLA leave are required to provide 30-day advance notice of the need to take FMLA leave when the need is foreseeable and such notice is practicable.

Employers may also require employees to provide:

- medical certification supporting the need for leave due to a serious health condition affecting the employee or an immediate family member;
- second or third medical opinions (at the employer's expense) and periodic recertification; **and**

- periodic reports during FMLA leave regarding the employee's status and intent to return to work.

When intermittent leave is needed to care for an immediate family member or the employee's own illness, and is for planned medical treatment, the employee must try to schedule treatment so as not to unduly disrupt the employer's operation.

Covered employers must post a notice approved by the Secretary of Labor explaining rights and responsibilities under FMLA. An employer that willfully violates this posting requirement may be subject to a fine of up to $100 for each separate offense.

Also, covered employers must inform employees of their rights and responsibilities under FMLA, including giving specific written information on what is required of the employee and what might happen in certain circumstances, such as if the employee fails to return to work after FMLA leave.

UNLAWFUL ACTS

It is unlawful for any employer to interfere with, restrain, or deny the exercise of any right provided by FMLA. It is also unlawful for an employer to discharge or discriminate against any individual for opposing any practice, or because of involvement in any proceeding, related to FMLA.

ENFORCEMENT

The Wage and Hour Division investigates complaints. If violations cannot be satisfactorily resolved, the U.S. Department of Labor may bring action in court to compel compliance. Individuals may also bring a private civil action against an employer for violations.

OTHER PROVISIONS

Special rules apply to **employees of local education agencies**. Generally, these rules provide for FMLA leave to be taken in blocks of time when intermittent leave is needed or the leave is required near the end of a school term.

Salaried executive, administrative, and professional employees of covered employers who meet the Fair Labor Standards Act (FLSA) criteria for exemption from minimum wage and overtime under Regulations, 29 CFR Part 541, do not lose their FLSA-exempt status by using any unpaid FMLA leave. This special exception to the "salary basis" requirements for FLSA's exemption extends only to "eligible" employees' use of leave required by FMLA.

The FMLA does not affect any other federal or state law which prohibits discrimination, nor supersede any state or local law which provides greater family or medical leave protection. Nor does it affect an employer's obligation to provide greater leave rights under a collective bargaining agreement or employment benefit plan. The FMLA also encourages employers to provide more generous leave rights.

FURTHER INFORMATION

The final rule implementing FMLA is contained in the January 6, 1995, Federal Register. For more information, please contact the nearest office of the **Wage and Hour Division**, listed in most telephone directories under U.S. Government, Department of Labor.

U.S. Department of Labor
Frances Perkins Building
200 Constitution Avenue, NW
Washington, DC 20210

1-866-4-USWAGE, TTY: 1-877-889-5627
Contact Us

Certification of Health Care Provider
(Family and Medical Leave Act of 1993)

U.S. Department of Labor
Employment Standards Administration
Wage and Hour Division

*(When completed, this form goes to the employee, **Not to the Department of Labor**.)*	OMB No.: 1215-0181 Expires: 08-31-2007

1. Employee's Name	2. Patient's Name *(If different from employee)*

3. Page 4 describes what is meant by a **"serious health condition"** under the Family and Medical Leave Act. Does the patient's condition[1] qualify under any of the categories described? If so, please check the applicable category.

(1) _____ (2) _____ (3) _____ (4) _____ (5) _____ (6) _____ , or None of the above _____

4. Describe the **medical facts** which support your certification, including a brief statement as to how the medical facts meet the criteria of one of these categories:

5. a. State the approximate **date** the condition commenced, and the probable duration of the condition (and also the probable duration of the patient's present **incapacity**[2] if different):

  b. Will it be necessary for the employee to take work only **intermittently or to work on a less than full schedule** as a result of the condition (including for treatment described in Item 6 below)?

   If yes, give the probable duration:

  c. If the condition is a **chronic condition** (condition #4) or **pregnancy**, state whether the patient is presently incapacitated[2] and the likely duration and frequency of **episodes of incapacity**[2]:

---

[1] Here and elsewhere on this form, the information sought relates **only** to the condition for which the employee is taking FMLA leave.

[2] "Incapacity," for purposes of FMLA, is defined to mean inability to work, attend school or perform other regular daily activities due to the serious health condition, treatment therefor, or recovery therefrom.

Form WH-380
Revised December 1999

6. a. If additional **treatments** will be required for the condition, provide an estimate of the probable number of such treatments.

If the patient will be absent from work or other daily activities because of **treatment** on an **intermittent** or **part-time** basis, also provide an estimate of the probable number of and interval between such treatments, actual or estimated dates of treatment if known, and period required for recovery if any:

b. If any of these treatments will be provided by **another provider of health services** (e.g., physical therapist), please state the nature of the treatments:

c. **If a regimen of continuing treatment** by the patient is required under your supervision, provide a general description of such regimen (*e.g.*, prescription drugs, physical therapy requiring special equipment):

7. a. If medical leave is required for the employee's **absence from work** because of the **employee's own condition** (including absences due to pregnancy or a chronic condition), is the employee **unable to perform work** of any kind?

b. If able to perform some work, is the employee **unable to perform any one or more of the essential functions of the employee's job** (the employee or the employer should supply you with information about the essential job functions)? If yes, please list the essential functions the employee is unable to perform:

c. If neither a. nor b. applies, is it necessary for the employee to be **absent from work for treatment**?

8. a. If leave is required to **care for a family member** of the employee with a serious health condition, **does the patient require assistance** for basic medical or personal needs or safety, or for transportation?

   b. If no, would the employee's presence to provide **psychological comfort** be beneficial to the patient or assist in the patient's recovery?

   c. If the patient will need care only **intermittently** or on a part-time basis, please indicate the probable **duration** of this need:

Signature of Health Care Provider   Type of Practice

Address   Telephone Number

       Date

To be completed by the employee needing family leave to care for a family member:

State the care you will provide and an estimate of the period during which care will be provided, including a schedule if leave is to be taken intermittently or if it will be necessary for you to work less than a full schedule:

Employee Signature   Date

A **"Serious Health Condition"** means an illness, injury impairment, or physical or mental condition that involves one of the following:

1. Hospital Care

   Inpatient care (*i.e.*, an overnight stay) in a hospital, hospice, or residential medical care facility, including any period of incapacity[2] or subsequent treatment in connection with or consequent to such inpatient care.

2. Absence Plus Treatment

   (a) A period of incapacity[2] of **more than three consecutive calendar days** (including any subsequent treatment or period of incapacity[2] relating to the same condition), that also involves:

      (1) **Treatment**[3] **two or more times** by a health care provider, by a nurse or physician's assistant under direct supervision of a health care provider, or by a provider of health care services (*e.g.*, physical therapist) under orders of, or on referral by, a health care provider; or

      (2) **Treatment** by a health care provider on **at least one occasion** which results in a **regimen of continuing treatment**[4] under the supervision of the health care provider.

3. Pregnancy

   Any period of incapacity due to **pregnancy**, or for **prenatal care**.

4. Chronic Conditions Requiring Treatments

   A **chronic condition** which:

      (1) Requires **periodic visits** for treatment by a health care provider, or by a nurse or physician's assistant under direct supervision of a health care provider;

      (2) Continues over an **extended period of time** (including recurring episodes of a single underlying condition); and

      (3) May cause **episodic** rather than a continuing period of incapacity[2] (*e.g.*, asthma, diabetes, epilepsy, etc.).

5. Permanent/Long-term Conditions Requiring Supervision

   A period of **Incapacity**[2] which is **permanent or long-term** due to a condition for which treatment may not be effective. The employee or family member must be **under the continuing supervision of, but need not be receiving active treatment by, a health care provider**. Examples include Alzheimer's, a severe stroke, or the terminal stages of a disease.

6. Multiple Treatments (Non-Chronic Conditions)

   Any period of absence to receive **multiple treatments** (including any period of recovery therefrom) by a health care provider or by a provider of health care services under orders of, or on referral by, a health care provider, either for **restorative surgery** after an accident or other injury, **or** for a condition that **would likely result in a period of Incapacity**[2] **of more than three consecutive calendar days in the absence of medical intervention or treatment**, such as cancer (chemotherapy, radiation, etc.), severe arthritis (physical therapy), and kidney disease (dialysis).

This optional form may be used by employees to satisfy a mandatory requirement to furnish a medical certification (when requested) from a health care provider, including second or third opinions and recertification (29 CFR 825.306).

Note: Persons are not required to respond to this collection of information unless it displays a currently valid OMB control number.

---

[3] Treatment includes examinations to determine if a serious health condition exists and evaluations of the condition. Treatment does not include routine physical examinations, eye examinations, or dental examinations.

[4] A regimen of continuing treatment includes, for example, a course of prescription medication (*e.g.*, an antibiotic) or therapy requiring special equipment to resolve or alleviate the health condition. A regimen of treatment does not include the taking of over-the-counter medications such as aspirin, antihistamines, or salves; or bed-rest, drinking fluids, exercise, and other similar activities that can be initiated without a visit to a health care provider.

Public Burden Statement

We estimate that it will take an average of 20 minutes to complete this collection of information, including the time for reviewing instructions, searching existing data sources, gathering and maintaining the data needed, and completing and reviewing the collection of information. If you have any comments regarding this burden estimate or any other aspect of this collection of information, including suggestions for reducing this burden, send them to the Administrator, Wage and Hour Division, Department of Labor, Room S-3502, 200 Constitution Avenue, N.W., Washington, D.C. 20210.

DO NOT SEND THE COMPLETED FORM TO THIS OFFICE; IT GOES TO THE EMPLOYEE.

Employer Response to Employee
Request for Family or Medical Leave
(Optional Use Form -- See 29 CFR § 825.301)

U.S. Department of Labor
Employment Standards Administration
Wage and Hour Division

(Family and Medical Leave Act of 1993)

Date:

OMB No. : 1215-0181
Expires : 08-31-07

To: _____
(Employee's Name)

From: _____
(Name of Appropriate Employer Representative)

Subject: **REQUEST FOR FAMILY/MEDICAL LEAVE**

On _____ , you notified us of your need to take family/medical leave due to:
(Date)

• The birth of a child, or the placement of a child with you for adoption or foster care; or

• • A serious health condition that makes you unable to perform the essential functions for your job: or

• • A serious health condition affecting your • spouse, • •child, • parent, for which you are needed to provide care.

You notified us that you need this leave beginning on _____ and that you expect
(Date)

leave to continue until on or about _____ .
(Date)

Except as explained below, you have a right under the FMLA for up to 12 weeks of unpaid leave in a 12-month period for the reasons listed above. Also, your health benefits must be maintained during any period of unpaid leave under the same conditions as if you continued to work, and you must be reinstated to the same or an equivalent job with the same pay, benefits, and terms and conditions of employment on your return from leave. If you do not return to work following FMLA leave for a reason other than: (1) the continuation, recurrence, or onset of a serious health condition which would entitle you to FMLA leave; or (2) other circumstances beyond your control, you may be required to reimburse us for our share of health insurance premiums paid on your behalf during your FMLA leave.

This is to inform you that: *(check appropriate boxes; explain where indicated)*

1. You are • eligible • not eligible for leave under the FMLA.

---

2. The requested leave • will • will not be counted against your annual FMLA leave entitlement.

---

3. You • will • will not be required to furnish medical certification of a serious health condition. If required, you must furnish certification by _____ *(insert date)* **(must be at least 15 days** after you are notified of this requirement), or we may delay the commencement of your leave until the certification is submitted.

---

4. You may elect to substitute accrued paid leave for unpaid FMLA leave. We • will • will not require that you substitute accrued paid leave for unpaid FMLA leave. If paid leave will be used, the following conditions will apply: *(Explain)*

Form WH-381
Rev. June 1997

5. (a) If you normally pay a portion of the premiums for your health insurance, these payments will continue during the period of FMLA leave. Arrangements for payment have been discussed with you, and it is agreed that you will make premium payments as follows: *(Set forth dates, e.g., the 10th of each month, or pay periods, etc. that specifically cover the agreement with the employee.)*

(b) You have a minimum 30-day *(or, indicate longer period, if applicable)* grace period in which to make premium payments. If payment is not made timely, your group health insurance may be cancelled, *provided* we notify you in writing at least 15 days before the date that your health coverage will lapse, or, at our option, we may pay your share of the premiums during FMLA leave, and recover these payments from you upon your return to work. We • will • will not pay your share of health insurance premiums while you are on leave.

(c) We • will • will not do the same with other benefits *(e.g., life insurance, disability insurance, etc.)* while you are on FMLA leave. If we do pay your premiums for other benefits, when you return from leave you • will • will not be expected to reimburse us for the payments made on your behalf.

6. You • will • will not be required to present a fitness-for-duty certificate prior to being restored to employment. If such certification is required but not received, your return to work may be delayed until certification is provided.

7. (a) You • are • are not a "key employee" as described in § 825.217 of the FMLA regulations. If you are a "key employee:" restoration to employment may be denied following FMLA leave on the grounds that such restoration will cause substantial and grievous economic injury to us as discussed in § 825.218.

(b) We • have • have not determined that restoring you to employment at the conclusion of FMLA leave will cause substantial and grievous economic harm to *us. (Explain (a) and/or (b) below. See §825.219 of the FMLA regulations.)*

8. While on leave, you • will • will not be required to furnish us with periodic reports every _____ _____ *(indicate interval of periodic reports, as appropriate for the particular leave situation)* of your status and intent to return to work *(see § 825.309 of the FMLA regulations)*. If the circumstances of your leave change and you are able to return to work earlier than the date indicated on the reverse side of this form, you • will • will not be required to notify us at least two work days prior to the date you intend to report to work.

9. You • will • will not be required to furnish recertification relating to a serious health condition. *(Explain below. if necessary, including the interval between certifications as prescribed in §825.308 of the FMLA regulations.)*

This optional use form may be used to satisfy mandatory employer requirements to provide employees taking FMLA leave with Written notice detailing spectfic expectations and obligations of the employee and explaining any consequences of a failure to meet these obligations. (29 CFR 825.301(b).)

Note: Persons are not required to respond to this collection of information unless it displays a currently valid OMB control number.

Public Burden Statement

We estimate that it will take an average of 5 minutes to complete this collection of information, including the time for reviewing instructions. searching existing data sources, gathering and maintaining the data needed, and completing and reviewing the collection of information. If you have any comments regarding this burden estimate or any other aspect of this collection of information, including suggestions for reducing this burden. send them to the Administrator, Wage and Hour Division, Department of Labor, Room S-3502. 200 Constitution Avenue, N.W., Washington. D.C. 20210.

DO NOT SEND THE COMPLETED FORM TO THE OFFICE SHOWN ABOVE.

Disability Report-Adult-Form SSA-3368-BK

DISABILITY REPORT - ADULT - Form SSA-3368-BK

PLEASE READ ALL OF THIS INFORMATION BEFORE YOU BEGIN
COMPLETING THIS FORM

THIS IS NOT AN APPLICATION

IF YOU NEED HELP

If you need help with this form, do as much of it as you can, and your interviewer will help you finish it. However, if you have access to the Internet, you may access the Disability Report Form Guide at http://www.socialsecurity.gov/disability/3368/index.htm.

HOW TO COMPLETE THIS FORM

The information that you give us on this form will be used by the office that makes the disability decision on your disability claim. You can help them by completing as much of the form as you can.

- Please fill out as much of this form as you can before your interview appointment.
- Print or type.
- **DO NOT LEAVE ANSWERS BLANK.** If you do not know the answers, or the answer is "none" or "does not apply," please write: "don't know," or "none," or "does not apply."
- **IN SECTION 4, PUT INFORMATION ON ONLY ONE DOCTOR/HOSPITAL/CLINIC IN EACH SPACE.**
- Each address should include a ZIP code. Each telephone number should include an area code.
- **DO NOT ASK A DOCTOR OR HOSPITAL TO COMPLETE THE FORM.** However, you can get help from other people, like a friend or family member.
- If your appointment is for an interview by telephone, have the form ready to discuss with us when we call you.
- If your appointment is for an interview in our office, bring the completed form with you or mail it ahead of time, if you were told to do so.
- When a question refers to "you," "your" or the "Disabled Person," it refers to the person who is applying for disability benefits. If you are filling out the form for someone else, please provide information about him or her.
- Be sure to explain an answer if the question asks for an explanation, or if you want to give additional information.
- If you need more space to answer any questions or want to tell us more about an answer, please use the "REMARKS" section on Pages 9 and 10, and show the number of the question being answered.

ABOUT YOUR MEDICAL RECORDS

If you have any medical records and copies of prescriptions at home for the person who is applying for disability benefits, send them to our office with your completed forms or bring them with you to your interview. Also, bring any prescription bottles with you. If you need the records back, tell us and we will photocopy them and return them to you.

YOU DO NOT NEED TO ASK DOCTORS OR HOSPITALS FOR ANY MEDICAL RECORDS THAT YOU DO NOT ALREADY HAVE. With your permission, we will do that for you. The information we ask for on this form tells us to whom we should send a request for medical and other records. If you cannot remember the names and addresses of any of the doctors or hospitals, or the dates of treatment, perhaps you can get this information from the telephone book, or from medical bills, prescriptions and prescription bottles.

WHAT WE MEAN BY "DISABILITY"

"Disability" under Social Security is based on your inability to work. For purposes of this claim, we want you to understand that "disability" means that you are unable to work as defined by the Social Security Act. You will be considered disabled if you are unable to do any kind of work for which you are suited and if your disability is expected to last (or has lasted) for at least a year or to result in death. So when we ask, "when did you become unable to work," we are asking when you became disabled as defined by the Social Security Act.

The Privacy And Paperwork Reduction Acts

The Social Security Administration is authorized to collect the information on this form under sections 205(a), 223(d) and 1631(e)(1) of the Social Security Act. The information on this form is needed by Social Security to make a decision on the named claimant's claim. While giving us the information on this form is voluntary, failure to provide all or part of the requested information could prevent an accurate or timely decision on the named claimant's claim. Although the information you furnish is almost never used for any purpose other than making a determination about the claimant's disability, such information may be disclosed by the Social Security Administration as follows: (1) to enable a third party or agency to assist Social Security in establishing rights to Social Security benefits and/or coverage; (2) to comply with Federal Laws requiring the release of information from Social Security records (e.g., to the General Accounting Office and the Department of Veterans Affairs); and (3) to facilitate statistical research and such activities necessary to assure the integrity and improvement of the Social Security programs (e.g., to the Bureau of the Census and private concerns under contract to Social Security).

We may also use the information you give us when we match records by computer. Matching programs compare our records with those of other Federal, State, or local government agencies. Many agencies may use matching programs to find or prove that a person qualifies for benefits paid by the Federal government. The law allows us to do this even if you do not agree to it.

Explanations about these and other reasons why information you provide us may be used or given out are available in Social Security offices. If you want to learn more about this, contact any Social Security office.

PAPERWORK REDUCTION ACT: This information collection meets the requirements of 44 U.S.C. § 3507, as amended by Section 2 of the Paperwork Reduction Act of 1995. You do not need to answer these questions unless we display a valid Office of Management and Budget control number. We estimate that it will take about 60 minutes to read the instructions, gather the facts, and answer the questions. **SEND OR BRING THE COMPLETED FORM TO YOUR LOCAL SOCIAL SECURITY OFFICE. The office is listed under U. S. Government agencies in your telephone directory or you may call Social Security at 1-800-772-1213.** *You may send comments on our time estimate above to: SSA, 1338 Annex Building, Baltimore, MD 21235-0001. Send only comments relating to our time estimate to this address, not the completed form.*

PLEASE REMOVE THIS SHEET BEFORE RETURNING THE COMPLETED FORM.

SOCIAL SECURITY ADMINISTRATION

Form Approved
OMB No. 0960-0579

DISABILITY REPORT
ADULT

For SSA Use Only
Do not write in this box.

Related SSN _____

Number Holder _____

SECTION 1- INFORMATION ABOUT THE DISABLED PERSON

A. **NAME** *(First, Middle Initial, Last)*

B. **SOCIAL SECURITY NUMBER**

C. **DAYTIME TELEPHONE NUMBER** *(If you have no number where you can be reached, give us a daytime number where we can leave a message for you.)*

_____ _____ ☐ Your Number ☐ Message Number ☐ None
Area
Code   Number

D. Give the name of a **friend or relative** that we can contact (other than your doctors) **who knows about your illnesses, injuries or conditions** and can help you with your claim.

NAME _____ RELATIONSHIP _____

ADDRESS _____
(Number, Street, Apt. No.(If any), P.O. Box, or Rural Route)

_____   DAYTIME _____
City   State   ZIP   PHONE   Area Code   Number

E. What is your **height** without shoes? _____ _____
feet   inches

F. What is your **weight** without shoes? _____
pounds

G. Do you have a **medical assistance card**? (For Example, Medicaid or Medi-Cal) If "YES," show the **number** here: ☐ YES ☐ NO
_____

H. Can you **speak and understand English**? ☐ YES ☐ NO   If "**NO**," what is your preferred language? _____

NOTE: If you cannot speak and understand English, we will provide an interpreter, free of charge.

If you cannot **speak and understand English**, is there someone we may contact who speaks and understands English and will give you messages? ☐ YES ☐ NO   *(If "YES," and that person is the same as in "D" above show "SAME" here. If not, complete the following information.)*

NAME _____ RELATIONSHIP _____
ADDRESS _____
(Number, Street, Apt. No.(If any), P.O. Box, or Rural Route)

_____   DAYTIME _____
City   State   ZIP   PHONE   Area Code   Number

I. Can you **read and understand English**? ☐ YES ☐ NO

J. Can you **write more than your name in English**? ☐ YES ☐ NO

FORM **SSA-3368-BK** (2-2004) EF (2-2004) Use 6-2003 edition Until Supply Exhausted

PAGE 1

Disability Report-Adult-Form SSA-3368-BK

SECTION 2
YOUR ILLNESSES, INJURIES OR CONDITIONS AND HOW THEY AFFECT YOU

A. What are the **illnesses, injuries or conditions** that limit your ability to work? _____

_____

B. How do your illnesses, injuries or conditions limit your ability to work? _____

_____

C. Do your illnesses, injuries or conditions cause you **pain**
or **other symptoms**? ☐ YES ☐ NO

D. When did your illnesses, injuries or conditions **first bother you**?

Month	Day	Year

E. When did you become **unable to work** because of your illnesses, injuries or conditions?

Month	Day	Year

F. Have you **ever worked**? ☐ YES ☐ NO *(If "NO," go to Section 4.)*

G. Did you **work at any time** after the date your illnesses, injuries or conditions first bothered you? ☐ YES ☐ NO

H. If "YES," did your illnesses, injuries or conditions cause you to: *(check all that apply)*

☐ work fewer hours? *(Explain below)*

☐ change your job duties? *(Explain below)*

☐ make any job-related changes such as your attendance, help needed, or employers? *(Explain below)*

_____

_____

_____

I. Are you **working now**? ☐ YES ☐ NO

If "NO," when did **you stop working**?

Month	Day	Year

J. Why did you **stop working**? _____

_____

_____

SECTION 3 - INFORMATION ABOUT YOUR WORK

A. List all the jobs that you had in the 15 years before you became unable to work because of your illnesses, injuries or conditions.

JOB TITLE (Example, Cook)	TYPE OF BUSINESS (Example, Restaurant)	DATES WORKED (month & year)		HOURS PER DAY	DAYS PER WEEK	RATE OF PAY (Per hour, day, week, month or year)	
		From	To				
						$	
						$	
						$	
						$	
						$	
						$	
						$	

B. Which job did you do the longest? _____

C. Describe this job. What did you do all day? (If you need more space, write in the "Remarks" section.) _____

D. In **this job**, did you:

Use machines, tools or equipment? ☐ YES ☐ NO

Use technical knowledge or skills? ☐ YES ☐ NO

Do any writing, complete reports, or perform duties like this? ☐ YES ☐ NO

E. In **this job**, how many total hours each day did you:

Walk? _____ Stoop? *(Bend down & forward at waist.)* _____ Handle, grab or grasp big objects? _____

Stand? _____ Kneel? *(Bend legs to rest on knees.)* _____ Reach? _____

Sit? _____ Crouch? *(Bend legs & back down & forward.)* _____ Write, type or handle small objects? _____

Climb? _____ Crawl? *(Move on hands & knees.)* _____

F. Lifting and Carrying *(Explain what you lifted, how far you carried it, and how often you did this.)* _____

G. Check **heaviest** weight lifted:

☐ Less than 10 lbs ☐ 10 lbs ☐ 20 lbs ☐ 50 lbs ☐ 100 lbs. or more ☐ Other _____

H. Check weight **frequently** lifted: *(By frequently, we mean from 1/3 to 2/3 of the workday.)*

☐ Less than 10 lbs ☐ 10 lbs ☐ 25 lbs ☐ 50 lbs. or more ☐ Other _____

I. Did you supervise other people in this job? ☐ YES (Complete items below.) ☐ NO (If NO, go to J.)

How many people did you supervise? _____

What part of your time was spent supervising people? _____

Did you hire and fire employees? ☐ YES ☐ NO

J. Were you a lead worker? ☐ YES ☐ NO

```
┌──────────────────────────────────────────────────────────┐
│     SECTION 4 - INFORMATION ABOUT YOUR MEDICAL RECORDS    │
└──────────────────────────────────────────────────────────┘
```

A. Have you been seen by a **doctor/hospital/clinic** or anyone else for the illnesses, injuries or conditions that limit your ability to work? ☐ YES ☐ NO

B. Have you been seen by a **doctor/hospital/clinic** or anyone else for emotional or mental problems that limit your ability to work? ☐ YES ☐ NO

If you answered "NO" to both of these questions, go to Section 5.

C. List **other names** you have used on your medical records. _____

_____

Tell us who may have medical records or other information about your illnesses, injuries or conditions.

D. List each **DOCTOR/HMO/THERAPIST/OTHER.** Include your **next appointment.**

1.
NAME		DATES
STREET ADDRESS		FIRST VISIT
CITY	STATE ZIP	LAST SEEN
PHONE Area Code Phone Number	PATIENT ID # (If known)	NEXT APPOINTMENT
REASONS FOR VISITS		
WHAT TREATMENT WAS RECEIVED?		

2.
NAME		DATES
STREET ADDRESS		FIRST VISIT
CITY	STATE ZIP	LAST SEEN
PHONE Area Code Phone Number	PATIENT ID # (If known)	NEXT APPOINTMENT
REASONS FOR VISITS		
WHAT TREATMENT WAS RECEIVED?		

SECTION 4 - INFORMATION ABOUT YOUR MEDICAL RECORDS

DOCTOR/HMO/THERAPIST/OTHER

3. NAME			DATES
STREET ADDRESS			FIRST VISIT
CITY	STATE	ZIP	LAST SEEN
PHONE *Area Code Phone Number*		PATIENT ID # (If known)	NEXT APPOINTMENT

REASONS FOR VISITS _____

WHAT TREATMENT WAS RECEIVED? _____

If you need more space, use Remarks, Section 9.

E. List each **HOSPITAL/CLINIC.** Include your **next appointment.**

1. HOSPITAL/CLINIC			TYPE OF VISIT	DATES	
NAME			☐ **INPATIENT** STAYS *(Stayed at least overnight)*	DATE IN	DATE OUT
STREET ADDRESS			☐ **OUTPATIENT** VISITS *(Sent home same day)*	DATE FIRST VISIT	DATE LAST VISIT
CITY	STATE	ZIP			
PHONE *Area Code Phone Number*			☐ **EMERGENCY ROOM** VISITS	DATE OF VISITS	

Next **appointment** _____ Your hospital/clinic **number** _____

Reasons for visits _____

What **treatment** did you receive? _____

What **doctors** do you see at this hospital/clinic on a regular basis? _____

SECTION 4-INFORMATION ABOUT YOUR MEDICAL RECORDS

HOSPITAL/CLINIC

2.	HOSPITAL/CLINIC			TYPE OF VISIT	DATES	
NAME				☐ **INPATIENT** STAYS *(Stayed at least overnight)*	DATE IN	DATE OUT
STREET ADDRESS				☐ **OUTPATIENT** VISITS *(Sent home same day)*	DATE FIRST VISIT	DATE LAST VISIT
CITY		STATE	ZIP	☐ **EMERGENCY ROOM** VISITS	DATE OF VISITS	
PHONE Area Code Phone Number						

Next **appointment** _____ Your hospital/clinic **number** _____

Reasons for visits _____

_____

What **treatment** did you receive? _____

_____

What **doctors** do you see at this hospital/clinic on a regular basis? _____

_____

If you need more space, use Remarks, Section 9.

F. Does **anyone else have medical records or information** about your illnesses, injuries or conditions (Workers' Compensation, insurance companies, prisons, attorneys, welfare), or are you scheduled to see anyone else?

☐ YES *(If "YES," complete information below.)*   ☐ NO

NAME	
	DATES
STREET ADDRESS	**FIRST** VISIT
CITY STATE ZIP	**LAST** SEEN
PHONE Area Code Phone Number	NEXT APPOINTMENT
CLAIM NUMBER (If any) _____	
REASONS FOR VISITS _____	

If you need more space, use Remarks, Section 9.

SECTION 5 - MEDICATIONS

Do you currently take any **medications** for your illnesses, injuries or conditions? ☐ YES

If "YES," please tell us the following: *(Look at your medicine bottles, if necessary.)* ☐ NO

NAME OF MEDICINE	IF PRESCRIBED, GIVE NAME OF DOCTOR	REASON FOR MEDICINE	SIDE EFFECTS YOU HAVE

If you need more space, use Remarks, Section 9.

SECTION 6 - TESTS

Have you had, or will you have, any **medical tests** for illnesses, injuries or conditions?

☐ YES ☐ NO   If "YES," please tell us the following: *(Give approximate dates, if necessary.)*

KIND OF TEST	WHEN DONE, OR WHEN WILL IT BE DONE? (Month, day, year)	WHERE DONE? (Name of Facility)	WHO SENT YOU FOR THIS TEST?
EKG (HEART TEST)			
TREADMILL (EXERCISE TEST)			
CARDIAC CATHETERIZATION			
BIOPSY--Name of body part			
HEARING TEST			
SPEECH/LANGUAGE TEST			
VISION TEST			
IQ TESTING			
EEG (BRAIN WAVE TEST)			
HIV TEST			
BLOOD TEST (NOT HIV)			
BREATHING TEST			
X-RAY--Name of body part _____			
MRI/CT SCAN Name of body part _____			

If you have had other tests, list them in Remarks, Section 9.

SECTION 7-EDUCATION/TRAINING INFORMATION

A. Check the highest grade of **school** completed.

Grade school: College:

0	1	2	3	4	5	6	7	8	9	10	11	12	GED		1	2	3	4 or more
☐	☐	☐	☐	☐	☐	☐	☐	☐	☐	☐	☐	☐	☐		☐	☐	☐	☐

Approximate **date** completed: _____

B. Did you attend **special education** classes? ☐ YES ☐ NO *(If "NO," go to part C)*

NAME OF SCHOOL _____

ADDRESS _____
(Number, Street, Apt. No.(if any), P.O. Box or Rural Route)

_____
City   State   Zip

DATES ATTENDED _____ TO _____

TYPE OF PROGRAM _____

C. Have you completed any type of **special job training, trade or vocational school?**

☐ YES ☐ NO If "YES," what type? _____

Approximate date completed: _____

**SECTION 8 - VOCATIONAL REHABILITATION, EMPLOYMENT,
or OTHER SUPPORT SERVICES INFORMATION**

Are you participating in the Ticket Program or another program of vocational rehabilitation services, employment services or other support services to help you go to work?

☐ YES (Complete the information below)   ☐ NO

NAME OF ORGANIZATION _____

NAME OF COUNSELOR _____

ADDRESS _____
(Number, Street, Apt. No.(if any), P.O. Box or Rural Route)

_____
City   State   Zip

DAYTIME PHONE NUMBER _____ _____
Area Code   Number

DATES SEEN _____ TO _____

TYPE OF SERVICES OR
TESTS PERFORMED   *(IQ, vision, physicals, hearing, workshops, etc.)*

SECTION 9 - REMARKS

Use this section for any added information you did not show in earlier parts of the form. When you are done with this section (or if you don't have anything to add), be sure to go to the next page and complete the blocks there.

SECTION 9 - REMARKS

_____

_____

_____

_____

_____

_____

_____

_____

_____

_____

_____

_____

_____

_____

_____

_____

_____

_____

_____

_____

_____

_____

_____

_____

_____

_____

_____

Name of person completing this form *(Please Print)*	**Date Form Completed** *(Month, day, year)*
Address *(Number and street)*	**e-mail address** *(optional)*
City **State**	**Zip Code**

WHOSE *Records to be Disclosed*	Form Approved OMB No. 0960-0623
NAME *(First, Middle, Last)*	
SSN _ _ _ _	Birthday *(mm/dd/yy)*

AUTHORIZATION TO DISCLOSE INFORMATION TO
THE SOCIAL SECURITY ADMINISTRATION (SSA)

** PLEASE READ THE ENTIRE FORM, BOTH PAGES, BEFORE SIGNING BELOW **

I voluntarily authorize and request disclosure (including paper, oral, and electronic interchange):

OF WHAT   *All my medical records;* also education records and other information related to my ability to perform tasks. This includes specific permission to release:

1. All records and other information regarding my treatment, hospitalization, and outpatient care for my impairment(s) *including*, and *not limited to*:
   -- Psychological, psychiatric or other mental impairment(s) (excludes "psychotherapy notes" as defined in 45 CFR 164.501)
   -- Drug abuse, alcoholism, or other substance abuse
   -- Sickle cell anemia
   -- Records which may indicate the presence of a communicable or venereal disease which may include, but are not limited to, diseases such as hepatitis, syphilis, gonorrhea and the human immunodeficiency virus, also known as Acquired Immune Deficiency Syndrome (AIDS); and tests for HIV.
   -- Gene-related impairments (including genetic test results)
2. Information about how my impairment(s) affects my ability to complete tasks and activities of daily living, and affects my ability to work.
3. Copies of educational tests or evaluations, including Individualized Educational Programs, triennial assessments, psychological and speech evaluations, and any other records that can help evaluate function; also teachers' observations and evaluations.
4. Information created within 12 months after the date this authorization is signed, as well as past information.

FROM WHOM

	THIS BOX TO BE COMPLETED BY SSA/DDS **(as needed)** Additional information to identify the subject (e.g., other names used), the specific source, or the material to be disclosed:
• **All medical sources** (hospitals, clinics, labs, physicians, psychologists, etc.) including mental health, correctional, addiction treatment, and VA health care facilities • All educational sources (schools, teachers, records administrators, counselors, etc.) • Social workers/rehabilitation counselors • Consulting examiners used by SSA • Employers • Others who may know about my condition (family, neighbors, friends, public officials)	

TO WHOM   The Social Security Administration and to the State agency authorized to process my case (usually called "disability determination services"), **including contract copy services, and doctors or other professionals consulted during the process.** [Also, for international claims, to the U.S. Department of State Foreign Service Post.]

PURPOSE   Determining my **eligibility for benefits**, including looking at the combined effect of any impairments that by themselves would not meet SSA's definition of disability; and whether I can manage such benefits.

☐ Determining whether I am **capable of managing benefits ONLY** (check only if this applies)

EXPIRES WHEN   This authorization is good for 12 months from the date signed (below my signature).

• I authorize the use of a copy (including electronic copy) of this form for the disclosure of the information described above.
• I understand that there are some circumstances in which this information may be redisclosed to other parties (see page 2 for details).
• I may write to SSA and my sources to revoke this authorization at any time (see page 2 for details).
• SSA will give me a copy of this form if I ask; I may ask the source to allow me to inspect or get a copy of material to be disclosed.
• I have read both pages of this form and agree to the disclosures above from the types of sources listed.

PLEASE SIGN USING BLUE OR BLACK INK ONLY	IF not signed by subject of disclosure, specify basis for authority to sign
INDIVIDUAL authorizing disclosure	☐ Parent of minor ☐ Guardian ☐ Other personal representative (explain)
SIGN ▶	(Parent/guardian/personal representative sign here if two signatures required by State law) ▶

Date Signed	Street Address		
Phone Number (with area code)	City	State	ZIP _

WITNESS   *I know the person signing this form or am satisfied of this person's identity:*

SIGN ▶	IF needed, second witness sign here (e.g., if signed with "X" above) **SIGN** ▶
Phone Number (or Address)	Phone Number (or Address)

This general and special authorization to disclose was developed to comply with the provisions regarding disclosure of medical, educational, and other information under P.L. 104-191 ("HIPAA"); 45 CFR parts 160 and 164; 42 U.S. Code section 290dd-2; 42 CFR part 2; 38 U.S. Code section 7332; 38 CFR 1.475; 20 U.S. Code section 1232g ("FERPA"); 34 CFR parts 99 and 300; and State law.

Form **SSA-827** (6-2007) ef (06-2007) Use 2-2003 and Later Editions Until Supply is Exhausted   Page 1 of 2

Explanation of Form SSA-827,
"Authorization to Disclose Information to the Social Security Administration (SSA)"

We need your written authorization to help get the information required to process your claim, and to determine your capability of managing benefits. Laws and regulations require that sources of personal information have a signed authorization before releasing it to us. Also, laws require specific authorization for the release of information about certain conditions and from educational sources.

You can provide this authorization by signing a form SSA-827. Federal law permits sources with information about you to release that information if you sign a single authorization to release all your information from all your possible sources. We will make copies of it for each source. A covered entity (that is, a source of medical information about you) may not condition treatment, payment, enrollment, or eligibility for benefits on whether you sign this authorization form. A few States, and some individual sources of information, require that the authorization specifically name the source that you authorize to release personal information. In those cases, we may ask you to sign one authorization for each source and we may contact you again if we need you to sign more authorizations.

You have the right to revoke this authorization at any time, except to the extent a source of information has already relied on it to take an action. To revoke, send a written statement to any Social Security Office. If you do, also send a copy directly to any of your sources that you no longer wish to disclose information about you; SSA can tell you if we identified any sources you didn't tell us about. SSA may use information disclosed prior to revocation to decide your claim.

It is SSA's policy to provide service to people with limited English proficiency in their native language or preferred mode of communication consistent with Executive Order 13166 (August 11, 2000) and the Individuals with Disabilities Education Act. SSA makes every reasonable effort to ensure that the information in the SSA-827 is provided to you in your native or preferred language.

IMPORTANT INFORMATION, INCLUDING NOTICE REQUIRED BY THE PRIVACY ACT

All personal information collected by SSA is protected by the Privacy Act of 1974. Once medical information is disclosed to SSA, it is no longer protected by the health information privacy provisions of 45 CFR part 164 (mandated by the Health Insurance Portability and Accountability Act (HIPAA)). SSA retains personal information in strict adherence to the retention schedules established and maintained in conjunction with the National Archives and Records Administration. At the end of a record's useful life cycle, it is destroyed in accordance with the privacy provisions, as specified in 36 CFR part 1228.

SSA is authorized to collect the information on form SSA-827 by sections 205(a), 223(d)(5)(A), 1614(a)(3)(H)(i), 1631(d)(1) and 1631 (e)(1)(A) of the Social Security Act. We use the information obtained with this form to determine your eligibility, or continuing eligibility, for benefits, and your ability to manage any benefits received. This use usually includes review of the information by the State agency processing your case and quality control people in SSA. In some cases, your information may also be reviewed by SSA personnel that process your appeal of a decision, or by investigators to resolve allegations of fraud or abuse, and may be used in any related administrative, civil, or criminal proceedings.

Signing this form is voluntary, but failing to sign it, or revoking it before we receive necessary information, could prevent an accurate or timely decision on your claim, and could result in denial or loss of benefits. Although the information we obtain with this form is almost never used for any purpose other than those stated above, the information may be disclosed by SSA without your consent if authorized by Federal laws such as the Privacy Act and the Social Security Act. For example, SSA may disclose information:

1. To enable a third party (e.g., consulting physicians) or other government agency to assist SSA to establish rights to Social Security benefits and/or coverage;
2. Pursuant to law authorizing the release of information from Social Security records (e.g., to the Inspector General, to Federal or State benefit agencies or auditors, or to the Department of Veterans Affairs(VA));
3. For statistical research and audit activities necessary to ensure the integrity and improvement of the Social Security programs (e.g., to the Bureau of the Census and private concerns under contract with SSA).

SSA will not redisclose without proper prior written consent information: (1) relating to alcohol and/or drug abuse as covered in 42 CFR part 2, or (2) from educational records for a minor obtained under 34 CFR part 99 (Family Educational Rights and Privacy Act (FERPA)), or (3) regarding mental health, developmental disability, AIDS or HIV.

We may also use the information you give us when we match records by computer. Matching programs compare our records with those of other Federal, State, or local government agencies. Many agencies may use matching programs to find or prove that a person qualifies for benefits paid by the Federal government. The law allows us to do this even if you do not agree to it.

Explanations about possible reasons why information you provide us may be used or given out are available upon request from any Social Security Office.

PAPERWORK REDUCTION ACT

This information collection meets the requirements of 44 U.S.C. § 3507, as amended by Section 2 of the Paperwork Reduction Act of 1995. You do not need to answer these questions unless we display a valid Office of Management and Budget control number. We estimate that it will take about 10 minutes to read the instructions, gather the facts, and answer the questions. **SEND OR BRING IN THE COMPLETED FORM TO YOUR LOCAL SOCIAL SECURITY OFFICE. The office is listed under U. S. Government agencies in your telephone directory or you may call Social Security at 1-800-772-1213 (TTY 1-800-325-0778).** You may send comments on our time estimate above to: SSA, 6401 Security Blvd., Baltimore, MD 21235-6401. Send **only** comments relating to our time estimate to this address, not the completed form.

Index